Walking on Heads

Walking on Heads

my charming imposter: a cautionary tale

dania matiation

Copyright © 2012 Dania Matiation

All rights reserved. No part of this book may be reproduced by any mechanical, photographic, or electronic process, or in the form of a phonographic recording; nor may it be stored in a retrieval system, transmitted or otherwise be copied for public or private use—other than for "fair use" as brief quotations embodied in articles and reviews—without prior written permission of the author.

Library and Archives Canada Cataloguing in Publication

Matiation, Dania, 1949–2011
    Walking on heads / Dania Matiation.

ISBN 978-1-926991-08-5

    I. Title.

PS8626.A835W34 2012   C813'.6   C2011-907792-2

Copy Editor: Adriana van Leeuwen
Proofreaders: Elspeth Richmond and Kyle Hawke
Cover and Text Designer: Alisha Whitley

Printed in Canada on recycled paper.

Granville Island Publishing
212–1656 Duranleau St.
Vancouver, BC
Canada V6H 3S4
www.granvilleislandpublishing.com

To my daughters and step-daughters

Table of Contents

	Prologue	ix
1	Going Dutch	1
2	It Could Happen to You	9
3	Encore	13
4	Excess Baggage	25
5	Sitting on Black Seed	31
6	When the Horse is Dead, Get Off!	41
7	A Woman Scorned is Like a Rodeo Clown	45
8	Sixteen! Sixteen!	65
9	Never Let the Same Dog Bite You Twice	73
10	Travel Changes Nothing Except the Location	79
11	All Together Now	87
12	The Droste Effect	93
13	Everyone is a Citizen Journalist	99

14	A Real Man Never Hits a Woman	109
15	Six Foot Two, Eyes of Blue	113
16	Raise a Little Hell	119
17	Hero or Villain?	123
18	GJ is a Trompe l'Oeil	131
19	Tennis, Anyone?	145
20	Once a Cheater, Always a Cheater	151
21	Abcdefg	157
22	The Fine Print	167
23	Exit Stage Left	171
	Acknowledgements	187
	Muffin Soup & Echo	190
	Topics for Discussion	192
	Author Bio	194

Prologue

In painting, drawing and in photography, artists occasionally use the 'Droste Effect' to create a mind-twisting experience. This illusionary technique was popularized by the Dutch artist M.C. Escher and the Dutch cocoa company Droste's famous label from 1904 whereupon a nurse holds a plate with a cup of cocoa and a box of Droste cocoa powder, on the packaging of which one can see an identical image, recursively diminishing in size and perception.

* ✪ *

As I park myself in my home office, I take the weight off my feet and back to gaze out the French windows which frame my back garden. I am physically tired, but not quite caving in yet. My mind is more alert and more dependable than I would have predicted as my illness takes cracks at resolving itself. As my wingback chair considerately absorbs my body, I feel rushes triggered by the scene parading the beauty and the strength of my bamboo set amongst my clusters of rhododendrons before me. The bees and I are in resonance, taking pleasure in the new blooms, while the birds peck away at the moss between the stepping stones where my daughters used to play with their Transformers.

From my vantage point over my modest garden, two images uncoil and plant themselves on the surface of my memory. Sprouting from the mist of my nostalgia about the lush beauty of my backyard, I feel gratitude that I have birthed two remarkable daughters, who fertilized my heart with laughter and blossoming curiosity as well as inducting me into life as a full-fledged woman. Each of my girls was raised with both feet in the earth and, though we often giggled about the pretty stinkweeds that burrowed under the back fence like trolls, their love of nature was never daunted.

The second image that springs from my dreamy space is an echo of an habitual prophecy: those shifty little weeds will try to invade my garden space unless someone removes them soon. These phantom visitors are prolific burgundy-leaved creepers with delicate pink flowers on innocent purple stems... except these weeds in floral disguise are tricksters, mimicking their selected ecosystem. Under the earth, their twisty and invasive roots seek to displace my green canvas by taking advantage of its vulnerability. Invaders such as these multiply with a purpose, growing quickly and sending out ever smaller and daintier versions of themselves with no sign of stopping.

While meditating behind the mullioned panes, I concede that thanks to my tough experience, I have learned that some people are like these weeds. They step into loaned settings, where it is their practice to borrow from lush conditions where the living is easy. They disguise their motives and take advantage of their new hosts' exposed circumstances by posing as beneficial companions.

These trespassers walk all over thriving inhabitants and crowd their way into the most established and beautiful milieu that they can find to occupy. Some of us would grab at that life, if we could get away with it, and damn the consequences, except that most of us (that is, ninety-six percent of the human race) would not encroach on another's sanctuary and conceal our intentions unless our continued existence was at stake.

Prologue

Remarkably, real life can be stranger than fiction. Today, my sagacity, my self-respect and a surprising talent as a citizen journalist are my legacy. For as much time as I have to live, my garden, my precious surviving daughter and my close friendships offer retreat from more than simple intruding weeds. My inner and outer world have been 'Drosted' or tricked by a duet of life's harsh medical jokes and trod on by a present-day Dutch illusionist. I should have folded and let my physical challenges scream for my attention, but my mental power—both as the guardian of my heart and of my daughter's memory and as the guide for my grinding determination—commanded the purge from my world of the intruder, who did not expect to be facing the repercussions of arousing the scrapper in me.

My recollections are not directly related to the rogue cancers that took me to the edge of my life. Instead, they are about the international misfit who transplanted himself into my vulnerable family, insulting my survival with an even more deceitful, hidden and misshapen sickness.

My reflections prompt me to think about how, when I first met the Dutchman, he reminded me of fresh spring blooms. There was so much promise, for at least one season in the sun. Still, *het is altijd anders dan je denkt*—things are never what you think they are.

1
Going Dutch

Life is not a matter of holding good cards,
but sometimes, of playing a poor hand well.
— Jack London —

Dear reader: This a short but intense story, almost unbelievable in its layers of appalling details, which, if revealed one at a time like dealing out playing cards, would seem wretched enough but when spread out, they were scandalous in the way they barged into my life. The most remarkable element to me is how I did not let the casino of events diminish me. My tenacity was as much a revelation to me as it was to the man who thought I would be a soft touch. My story is about an ordinary person uniting with exceptional people to rise above extraordinary events.

Welcome to my world.

It all started when I allowed a dashing Dutchman to sweep me off my feet. Seriously—the first moment we touched hands, he lifted me up and swung me around with a deep trickle of melodic laughter and I adore laughter (particularly if it comes with a resonant voice and a gorgeous man).

I had freshly survived a complicated breakup after eight years of colliding with my partner, Jack, whom I'd thought of as my soul mate but who had decided the grass was greener with another. I had propped my body and headspace back together and was open and ready for consensual fun.

Walking on Heads

My kids were full-grown, my hair was still soft brown, I could do a wicked shimmy and I was confident about the future, not scrounging for a storybook ending like some women I knew. My daughters and I called ourselves the 'Three Little Maids', after the Gilbert and Sullivan tune that well described the joy and lightness that was our little family. We three maids made adventures of our detours due to financial status, which in the end made us all very flexible and adaptable. Once the girls were able to get behind the wheel of a car and drive, the fourth maid became our vehicle, which we always named according to its licence plate letters. We called the car I have now Bullwinkle, which tells you a bit about our collective imagination and united buoyancy.

However, my single life was so busy with my work as a teacher, my piety to motherhood and my various recreational activities, that I dared to resort to what my daughters claimed was *the* way to meet new people who also wanted to avoid the bar scene. My girls assured me that it was done by many of their friends, particularly if they were new to town or too occupied with their studies or their careers. My daughters were totally behind me, to the point of finding me a quality guy who was looking for a fine woman.

What was a girl to do but go with the social flow? I took to internet dating introductions, where I felt like a teenager in a candy shop. According to 2011 stats, one in five singles—no matter what their colour, age, religious background or sexual preference—venture at some point to a dating service. So it seemed like an innocent way to screen the mix-and-mingle potential. I started to peek and flirt on a well-known singles site.

Not that age has anything to do with emotional status or emotional miscalculations or emotional vulnerability. I just simply dissolved for the fourth man I met on the introductions network.

The first, Richard, was my buddy for a couple of years. I dated Peter, the second volunteer, for a couple of months, but he was still smarting from being dumped by his wife of five years and we parted awkwardly because I didn't want to be the rebound for his attachment problems.

Going Dutch

Then, I met a handsome and brilliant writer who had an open relationship with his partner of several years. He was totally upfront, at least, but I chose to sneak out the back door of that complication.

Dutchcosmo, an intellectual, caught me in his spell almost immediately after I read his rundown. On his profile, he stood on a coastal beach in a navy jacket and white cotton trousers, looking every bit like the thoughtful academic he claimed to be.

Dutchcosmo and I winked and then e-mailed a couple of times, which (in case you don't know) is the rite of passage on dating sites. I surrendered a little of my background, interests and boundaries, and then had the elbow room to assess his responses. He wrote decent English as he told me about his passion for jogging, social democracy and Kipling, one of my favourite poets. Therefore, I bit the bullet and sent him my cellphone number.

It was at a coffee shop that same afternoon, with a tense blush and a nervous chortle, that I paraded his profile before a couple of my close girlfriends, Liz and Linsey. These dear friends and I had birthed our babies within a couple of years of each other and had raised the kids together until the children chose their own special friends, but these two women were still two of my very close companions. Between each of their eyebrows I saw stereo lines of concern, until I scrolled through his introduction on my smartphone and then flashed his photo. Each of my worldly—or maybe I should say 'seasoned'—friends looked patiently at me, no doubt thinking back to my breakups and tougher times. And then they crooned in unison, rallying their comments back and forth:

"Ooooh, now he could challenge your . . . mind . . . "

"What a gorgeous specimen . . . "

"What the hell, go for it, honey . . ."

" . . . Just keep us on speed-dial in case he's a psycho."

So, the enchantment germinated as the Dutchman and I shared words on the telephone for over an hour the next evening and dipped into each other's lives, doing the dance of introductions. It was effortless

Walking on Heads

to talk with him, although our backgrounds were very different. He had worked the world, while I had worked and enthralled the minds of captive students. Since I was dating Richard—who wasn't my romantic idol, but benignly kept me out of mischief—I was slow to immediately grant a face-to-face to Dutchcosmo.

I took my time, and he waited patiently.

I will call him Goos Jank, which is not his real name. Since I could not pronounce any of his names (and could not bring myself to call him Gerald, as he suggested), I went with GJ. He was born in the year with two fives in it. And you can think of me as Anni, pronounced ah-nee, which is my middle name, inherited from my Finnish grandmother. I was born in a year with two nines in it.

Two weeks after a number of telephone chats, during which I luxuriated in his accent, his deep voice and his beguiling words (not necessarily in that order), I agreed to meet GJ at a public location on a Thursday afternoon after my school day ended. I chose the place and time, which would allow me to spot him from my vantage point first. We decided to rendezvous at Lonsdale Quay on the north shore of my city, Vancouver, and then to play the conversation shell game over a glass of wine. I am a visual processor as well as a visual learner and I knew that the last test, as this unknown man headed my way off the little ferry, would be to take score of his eye contact with his environment (in other words, to watch for any shiftiness) and to see if his photo was up to date.

A man in a suit has such an aura of testosterone, power, emotional strength, trust or whatever our mental tape is. James Bond or a groom in his happiest hour seal the suit deal for me. As it happened, on the afternoon when GJ and I finally locked eyes, he was dressed in his Italian two-piece grey, en route to the dinner opening of the new Capilano University in North Vancouver as a representative of the Dutch government. There he was in suave attire: tall, silvery-blond and even more mystifying than his picture! He saw me and I saw him as he threaded his way off the SeaBus like an international jetsetter, looking gorgeous and friendly

Going Dutch

and honourable. I, on the other hand, was wearing an old but form-fitting blouse and corduroy jeans, straight from my workday at the school. Nevertheless, our smiles tumbled generously and we started our walk and talk.

Eventually we stopped for a glass of wine (Malbec for me and a goblet of Riesling for him) and lounged in an intimate Italian bistro, which catalyzed more exchanging of our souls. He told me about his work and I told him about my children (including my students) and my dream job, which allowed me to touch young minds with my stories on a variety of subjects that just happened to be part of the educational curriculum. What I didn't know was that he could tell stories very well and that they would romance and entice many of the people in my life, including myself. His first anecdote was that I reminded him of a past partner named Annelies, whom he regretted losing. I looked into his soft, sapphire eyes and a thought flashed, like Chinese fireworks, *I may have a chance with this guy!*

Then we took an unforgettable stroll along a waterfront that used to house shipyards. He walked with his arm protectively around my shoulder and laughed often and freely for the pure joy of being in my city. That was the Walt Disney moment, when he put air beneath my feet and stars swirling in my head. Needless to say, he had a vibrant freshness and twinkling blue eyes that seemed intended for me alone. I am not exactly naïve, so I simply thought this accented man could be an *amuse-bouche*. Therefore, when he told me he had two season's passes for the Grouse Grind hike and asked if I'd like to push him up the slope on the weekend, we agreed that our first date would be an uphill climb.

As it turned out, trekking with GJ through the forest turned into the most fun I had had in a while. We were both in shape, physically and mentally. He still played tennis and cycled, putting him in pretty good form for a weathered guy. And 'doing' the 2.9-kilometre uphill trail in North Vancouver can take your breath away as much as the beautiful landscape can. We puffed, laughed and stopped to pleasure ourselves with the frost-starched panorama as our conversation travelled around a

Walking on Heads

variety of topics. And my heart was starting to feel something for a man that it hadn't felt in a while, which was little flutters of eagerness.

I discovered that GJ spoke five languages fluently, which is not uncommon for someone from a small European country but somewhat rare for a Canadian. Then again, his mother had been Flemish and his father had been raised in Germany, so you can speculate on the fifth tongue. I spoke English and a little French, but although I studied Latin for four years, it had left the building, so to speak.

What was riveting for me was GJ's knowledge about humankind, especially the world of politics. His grasp of philosophy was doing something to my blood pressure, in a good way. I learned about the complexities of the Dutch affairs of state, with their many parties ranging from Calvinist to Communist, and how philosophers conclude that there is seldom one simple answer to a question. I loved how his mind touched mine.

I told him about my writing. I had just published a book on a topic very close to my heart, called *Motherwords*. My sacred prose contained stories and words of wisdom from my mother, her mother, my mother-in-law and from my own blithe insight. The book tour was set for the summer, and I was already doing a few book launches at local libraries.

He also seemed to be intrigued by how my thoughts were tickling his. I am an optimist and somewhat childlike in how I find amusement or grace in simple things. The hike felt like best friends out climbing to the top of their world.

When he described his civil service work in development aid with the Netherlands Ministry of Foreign Affairs, as a steadfast supporter of social justice, I was intellectually besotted and felt hot in my nether regions. When he mentioned his plan to buy a home on a Greek island (as a matter of fact, near the residence of a very well-loved Canadian poet and songwriter), I was intrigued. Even though I wasn't born yesterday, I have to admit that I made a sultry, throaty chant of the two words "Pinch me!" to his twinkling eyes, like I was doing an inner 'OM'. Weeks later, when

Going Dutch

he sighed that he wanted us to travel together one day and show me his Greece, I pinched myself several times.

From then on, I was rapt and exhilarated. GJ respectfully spoke about his Canadian roommate, Marie, who was his academic protégée and Canadian Ph.D student and was working with him on his Dutch project in the Balkans. Each time he came to my home or we met for a walk, he seemed charmingly mesmerized by me . . . but he took things slowly, or at least mirrored my pace. I gradually conceded that I had a crush!

As I got to know him, GJ continued to be the most thoughtful man I had known aside from my father, a breath of fresh air compared to some of the more self-centred men I had dated or even loved. GJ would tell me to stay in my seat while he cleared the table after dining. He was old-fashioned (or just European, as he would say), opening the car door for me when we went out, making sure that I was temperature-controlled and that I walked on the inside of the sidewalk when we sauntered through the city. He would shrug and say that it had something to do with having spent years below sea level on man-made polders—which are islands surrounded by dikes—in Holland. Whether that was true or not, he was a classic gentleman.

"Has anyone ever told you you're a fine woman?" he would frequently ask. Each time my reply would be, "Yes, as a matter of fact. Just . . . yesterday!"

So you see, potent beginnings are not just for teenagers. GJ was a not only a gentle man, but certainly the most alluring man I had kissed in a while. Despite the fact that he had been in the Balkans for several years and had seen post-traumatic stress horrors, he kept a light sense of sympathy and optimism about him. And that was sexy.

On top of that, he thought that I had an exquisitely gentle spirit and unfathomable mind. The first time he lightly declared, "Anni, you are one of the most sensitive yet strong women I have known—like a beautiful bamboo," I was touched. And when he said he loved my kaleidoscope eyes with their green and yellow and blue patterns and that he was

Walking on Heads

drawn to my warm heart and my intelligence, he vacuumed me up with his words and wrapped my spirit around his little finger. So you cannot blame me for beginning the relationship with an excellent sufficiency of optimism.

2
It Could Happen to You

*If you don't stand up for something,
you may fall for anything.*
— Malcolm X —

So here's the set-up. When GJ and I met, I was footloose (free from daily parenting duties, I mean) and grounded and calm within myself as a single woman. True, I was open to a new relationship, I will not tell a lie, but I was not unsettled, anxious or needy on that front. I had survived breast cancer for almost five years and I now caressed every day with gratitude for life's simple pleasures.

I lived comfortably in Vancouver, the western Canadian city known for its views of mountains and ocean and for its temperate weather. When my children were young, my daughters and I often walked to the beach from our house in Kitsilano to look for limpets, barnacles and the little crabs that would scatter and flee from under the rocks in the tidal pools. From our home, we could also pile into the car and easily drive up a mountain, telling each other stories or singing at the top of our lungs as we enjoyed our times together.

After the girls left home to live independently, I busied myself with my garden, meditation, Afro-Jazz dance classes, dates, my fabulous, funny, faithful friends and my top-notch teaching colleagues. My daughters,

Walking on Heads

Nathalie and Maxine, both lived across the harbour with their partners and were energized by their blossoming lives. Nat was a whimsical poet and journalism student, an avid and prolific reader, with a rich inner life which had originated when she was a daydreamy child who revelled in clandestine discussions and notes to and from Flora (her flower fairy) under the rhododendrons at age four. And Max was a talented musician, singer and songwriter who had been melodic from a very young age, sensing rhythms and singing often as she played with her toys. Max was studying at the Art Institute during the day and practicing or performing when she had time available on weekends. My two little maids relished working together for a landscaping firm during their summers off from school.

Even my relationships with my ex-husband Paul and my in-laws were comfortable. "Anni, made any of the sour red berry soup of your grandmother's lately?" Paul would often joke, since we both despised that soup. My children's father was still a part of my life, as indeed was Jack, the man I'd just surfaced from a fairly long-term relationship with. Both he and his daughters, as a matter of fact, were still important to my family.

There were few ghosts, goblins or ghouls breathing down my neck. One of those few was that Max had come out as a gay woman two years before and I felt very protective of her because there are some who think homosexuality is a disease or a birth defect or a deficiency of parenting. I worried about the kind of weirdoes who might mug her or discriminate against her. And second, to out-rankle that worry, my first-born, Nat, discovered a little lump in her right breast just a month after I started to fall for GJ and there was scarcely a place to go in my mind where I could avoid crashing into that reality.

GJ was a welcome breath of fresh air, given my duel with the way my comfortable life had been sideswiped by my daughters' issues. He was steadfast, tuned in to my ups and downs and he added a layer of fun and affection to the terrors squeezing and gouging my heart.

However, my inner compass was impatiently repelling me from this international relationship. I deliberated and juggled the truth, but I couldn't allow myself to grab at love and be whisked out of the country by this exceptional man. Part of the problem was that I knew for sure that it didn't feel right to be in a romance while my first-born was heading for surgery to save her from her skirmish with her health. I also felt that I could not follow GJ to Europe to 'walk on heads' (as the Dutch call manoeuvring through crowds) while my youngest babe was pioneering her new life as a young gay wife with the responsibility of supporting her Eastern European-immigrant spouse. That couple was facing more than your average financial and social challenges. I simply could not walk away and put my needs ahead of those of my children at that point.

In addition, on top of those significant details, key things were niggling at me about the handsome, wonderful GJ.

The first thing to prickle my antennae was that his ex-girlfriend from Portugal seemed to be running him down for money for her children. He had developed a tiny habit of teasing his outer eyebrows when his thoughts were wandering (and, I assumed, thinking about it). As a matter of fact, he flippantly told me, while we were setting the dining table one evening, that she called him often and that she was jealous because he had moved on. He moaned discourteously that she wanted him back to help with the care of her kids. Then he literally shrugged her off with a scrunch of his shoulders.

Added to that somewhat dismissive attitude was the second fact that GJ had never spent more than the cost of a glass of wine on me. I am not a princess, but I did think it was odd that everything we did was free and that we only ate together at my home from my pantry. In a corner of my mind, I thought he was a cheapskate and that was a fuzzy question mark hovering over him.

There was also some ambiguity about his possible move to Ireland to partner with researchers from the University of Limerick to finish his Balkan report. He had sort of asked me a couple of times if I would like to live there, but that plan was quite vague.

And with a heavy sigh, I admitted to myself that my last fixation was with the fact that GJ rarely spoke about his children. In fact, Christmas was approaching and he hadn't made plans to be with them or invite them to share Christmas with us. He hadn't seen—or, as far as I could figure out, talked with—either of his kids for months, yet he didn't seem to miss his boys. I was profoundly puzzled by his casual connection with his sons, because parenthood was a huge priority in my own life.

While comparing the pluses to the life-sized negatives one afternoon, I ate a huge bowl of tortilla chips in the wingback chair in my home office that I had occasionally used for private conversations when the girls were in residence. I was cocooned in my phoning headquarters in the midst of comfort consumption partly to dumb down my anxiety about my daughters and partly for the courage to ditch the man.

Armed with my shield of crumbs, I called him up and kindly awarded him his walking papers, counting the reasons as I massaged my left foot. Starting at the little toe with the fact that I couldn't possibly leave Nathalie, I moved on to the next digit and pointed out his confusion about his Portuguese friend. The middle toe represented his lack of clarity about Ireland, while my most beautiful toe got gently massaged as I pointed out the culture shock I felt because he hadn't taken me out (except for the Grouse Grind, with season's passes that were in his roommate's name). Mentioning his kids seemed like too low a blow, because I was the flag-bearer for parenthood, so I wiped my hands and big toe of him as I shook the chip crumbs from my clothing onto the floor. I cut GJ loose with a proud 'I am a strong woman!' inner stance.

Soon after that, I returned to occasionally seeing other men, including Richard. I seriously never pined for GJ, although a juvenile part of me did miss the exquisite sparkle that had enhanced the most beautiful blue eyes I had ever leaned towards. A teensy part of me also thought, *Damn it*.

3

Encore

Everything happens for a reason, even when we are not wise enough to see it.
— Oprah Winfrey —

Fast-forward six months, and my energy was in a vastly different space. I had enough experience to understand that life was complex and layered, but I had never, ever had to steep my heart in and choke on the truth of being the mother of a very sick child. I was relentlessly battling two separate emotions: love and anger.

For most parents, including Ms. Anni Mills, the ultimate worry is that their child might be deeply frightened, in pain, in trouble, or—worst of all—might die agonizingly alone before them.

And here's what happened. Unbeknownst to me, my eldest daughter Nathalie had found out that her cancer challenge had developed into an absurdly aggressive condition and had spread. At the same time, inside a week of her discovery that her cancer had found a new place to camp out, I thought that I might be developing asthma. Within a couple of days of Nat's own news, my doctor told me that the big 'C' was back, this time in my lung.

I did not consider it okay to spill the beans to Nathalie about my health update, because I wanted to protect her from having to worry about me. I wanted to preserve her energy for her own recovery. My poor girl had enough to deal with, as far as I was concerned, and she seemed to be pulling through her treatments well, looking at me as the principal example of expectant survival. I did not want her to lose hope, but the apple doesn't fall too far from the tree, given the fact that she didn't tell anyone about her additional diagnosis except her partner Rob, her best friend Chloe (who was in medical school) and Max . . . either to protect the family, or to wait until she had wrapped her mind around the medical reports.

Dear Maxine, who is my emotional child, was privy to both of our ghastly scenarios. At first, I didn't want to involve Max with my own delicate cancer encore either. It was hard enough for her to be worried about her sister's recovery, but I did have to own up as to why I was suddenly so scattered and emotional. Furthermore, I wanted her and her wife Liana to come with me to my first appointments, including my first lung drain. So it turned out that Max was in on both bizarre news flashes.

That was the most twisted week of my life, as details, procedures, phone calls and detours all came at me with dizzying speed. I was in a contest with my breathing, which was more an emotional kickback than a physical one. So, my dear friend Richard kidnapped me mid-week and dragged me out to dine with him. He had lost his wife five years before and he was understandably worried about me. "Hey, Anni, let me take you away. I'm better company than a bag of bath salts." He was such a good guy—he knew how to keep things upbeat and positive, which was one of the reasons I liked him so much.

From our favourite Stanley Park eatery, he ordered steak and veggies, while I had two seafood tacos—our regular, predictable choices. The beauty of this restaurant was that the paths surrounding the garden patio offered a vision of cyclists, walkers and rollerbladers—and the food was excellent. While we were just wrapping up our meal, both of our phones buzzed. His was a call from his son about their plans for the weekend, and mine was a text from Maxine which sent me flying out of the restaurant's double doors and past the tennis courts to my parked car with sweaty palms and teeth clenched. The six little words were "You and Nat need to talk! xo."

I cannot even go into our first conversation, except that with her trademark lilt, Nathalie softly said, "Mommy, I'm experiencing some technical difficulties!" Humour was always one of her strong suits . . . and being incredibly intelligent, like a walking Trivial Pursuit game . . . and being a head-turning beauty . . . and being an outside-the-box creative thinker . . .

. . . and being unwaveringly stoic.

What made no sense to any of us was that Nathalie had been a healthy home-birthed baby who had been breast-fed for two years. She had grown into an exuberant, outdoorsy girl who was athletic, organic and happy, with hopes and dreams for her future. She'd had the common experiences of teens, falling in and out of love, but the fact that her parents had split had never bruised or maimed her belief in the exhilarating days ahead. She was in a fabulous, extraordinary union with Rob, the love of her life and one of my heroes. She and her sister were great friends, had eaten the same food, breathed the same air, were adored by the same parents, but she was struck for no apparent reason and I thought it was stupid, stupid, stupid!

I stepped down immediately from my teaching position because I knew that I could not be the professional I had been before, not after the double verdict that had walloped my being and left me gasping for air. It wasn't fair to my students, the school district or the parents who had left their children in my care. My doctor advised me to give immediate notice to the principal administrator at our school and take care of my body as well as my spirit. Letting go of my job was bittersweet, because I loved my work, but it gave me the time and energy to spend a large portion of my weeks helping with transport to and from Nat's appointments and treatments. Nathalie's partner, Rob, had a high-pressure international job in logistics and he did as much as he could (which was the lion's share of committed tender care), but crises require a full-on team of loving hearts. In true form, my dear Nat was often apologetic for causing others to rearrange their days to help her out.

Dangling like an inchworm over all of our shoulders was a smarting in our family's soul and we needed to talk each other through our snowballing sorrow. We had a phalanx of family and friends who could take on parts of Nat's care or simply hang out with her. They were troopers, willing to let us whimper about our fears and to give her space, entertainment, helping hands or whatever else she wanted. It was a terrifying and enormously difficult time for us all, watching Nat slowly fade as our hearts twisted in misery. There seemed to be hardly any time to breathe, let alone believe in the future.

I don't remember how any of us managed to do any of the normal day-to-day things like housework, shopping or having fun. I checked in with Max and Liana regularly to be sure that they were handling the crises okay. It took every bit of acting talent that I had to pretend that I wasn't thoroughly drowning because of Nat's health and to avoid acknowledging that I had also been given the palliative verdict. It was also a clear priority to give Maxine my time and my attention and assure her that both she and Nat were enormously important to me. I needed to wear my words so that Max would have no doubt that neither darling daughter was more special to me. Nathalie simply needed our resources and attention during that time period.

I was also heaving inner sighs about Max and Liana's marriage, which was in its tricky fine-tuning phase. On top of our family's medical challenges, the couple were having cultural difficulties and financial pressures because of immigration rules that did not allow Liana to work, meaning Max was expected to support her for two years. Liana was bored and wanted to get back to her career in tennis coaching. And, being lesbians (or, more to the point, both female), there were occasional hormonal and emotional clashes. Trumping that, of course, they were scared shitless that Maxine might also be in danger of becoming the next cancer casualty.

Encore

The stressed out newlyweds were both only twenty, which seemed very young—or at least very hasty—when it came to their decision to run down the aisle, but their swift decision to marry was partly driven by their need to secure Liana's residence in Canada. Looking back, I realized I was also twenty when Paul and I married, while we were on our way to hike around Europe for a summer. And my own Mom was twenty when she and Dad eloped. I had to trust that they would find their own way.

So, while we were all rallying around Nathalie, we were also wrenching our nerves as we waited on our genetic testing results. Nat, Max, Liana, Paul and I were all petrified that Maxine possibly could be next in line, particularly since both of her grandmothers had dealt with stage-two breast cancers. I know that we all grew a few silver hairs while awaiting that verdict, and I took to annoying my cuticles. It was yet another extra cock-eyed piece twisting our headspace.

At this point in this story, magnificent news came as I was plating leftovers for lunch on a Monday. A nurse named Janet (who had interviewed and counselled our family with silky compassion) finally called and I was so glad that I was home to intercept her momentous announcement. Janet was perfectly and utterly overjoyed to share the test results, which gave us all massive, relieved exhalations and something to celebrate for the approaching year. We had been queasy and twisted in the bowels of our beings for months, but finally, we learned that Maxine did not have the mutation of her BRCA1 gene that both and Nat and I had. I sobbed with joy throughout the entire conversation. After ensuring that Max had picked up on her phone call and that she had received the message, I dropped in for a visit with dear Nathalie, whose colour was infinitely brightened by the news that her sister would be okay. Not only was Nat truly relieved, I didn't even see a wisp of a cloud of sadness for herself cross her face.

I hate the phrase 'everything happens for a reason'. However, whatever the universal game plan had in mind, I was on oral chemo and mostly oblivious to my own crisis. As if I should be the one awarded the get-out-of-jail-free card, I was responding well to my treatments and my condition was stable, so I forgot that I, too, was looking down the barrel of a gun. Nat's needs trumped my own and, in a way, that made most of my physical discomforts fade.

If this part of my story were a stage play, my diagnosis and Max's sexual orientation would only be props, like pieces of furniture, adding to the setting of the greater plot. Nat's diagnosis certainly would be the pathos, but the main theme would usurp the medical and parental dramas, adding a bizarrely rotated focus that no one could have seen coming.

What happened next was that in the midst of our family's hellish medical chaos, the Dutchman dropped back into my world. GJ let me know that he was still based in Vancouver for an indefinite period, and he sensed that I might be in need of some support. He reopened the conversation between us on Facebook, our favourite social network, with, "How is Nathalie?"

Again, I was transported back to those blue eyes, that deep voice and his yummy accent. Here he was, tuning in at time of need, showing interest and being considerate, caring and thoughtful!

I e-mailed him the verdict and placed optimism into my words, then changed the subject by asking him what he had been up to and what happened with Ireland. He said that the Irish economy had tanked and the university had no funding for international partnerships. He described reams of paperwork, including his next project outline. Then he wondered if there was anything he could do for us. I flippantly said, "Take me away to Greece!" and he replied, "Okay, when? . . . And what can I do also?"

If you were to meet GJ, you would come into contact with his magic as he mingled with you and listened and responded to your words. He would walk the line with intellect and style and seem to care deeply about your concerns and anxieties.

To break the ice a little more, he sent me a picture of a villa on the island of Zanzibar and asked if I would like to visit him there in the next year to work on the educational part of his project. I joked that my moral high ground didn't allow me to mingle with people who hired house staff, so I'd likely take a pass on living in a villa, but I was intrigued by his mission.

Unbelievably, the day that he reconnected with me, as I was driving to a massage appointment I saw a tall, gorgeous man who looked very much like him walking along Fourth Avenue holding hands with a petite blonde woman. Despite feeling very idiotic about my next move, I turned right and circled the block to look again, and for sure, that was him!

Surprisingly, he phoned me that evening asking how I was. I blubbered a few niceties and then blurted, "I thought I saw you strolling in my neighbourhood today, deeply engrossed in conversation with a woman." I was hoping that maybe his sister or relative was visiting from Holland, but he replied that he and his roommate Marie were heading back to her car after celebrating her birthday lunch.

"You were holding hands," I ventured.

Now, did you know that traditional European men often hold hands with women? He guaranteed that it was only a transitory thing, as Marie was sharing concerns about her love life and needed an anchor and a friend. I put that image into a file in my mind called 'Hmmm'.

From that conversation onwards, GJ started to become my anchor and showed enormous compassion, interest and willingness to be there for me, paying attention to my words, including all my wobbly dialogue, confusion and the fright of a mother losing her child.

Still, GJ was back and forth from Vancouver Island, and I was still to-ing and fro-ing from Nathalie and Rob's home and darting to appointments with Nat and lending a hand in coordinating her care.

Regardless of that, I was in no hurry to replay a relationship with GJ, so I had him chasing me for a few more weeks. And what woman doesn't like to be pursued? I know it's a primal thing, but it was endearing, so I eventually took a bit of a breather from my role with Nat, passed the baton to others on the team and waved my white silk panties in surrender to him.

I'll skim through the somewhat decent part of this story. GJ and I gradually started to see each other again, although we mostly talked on the telephone or by e-mail whenever we both had the time. I still had mammoth mothering responsibilities, and he had his job with the Netherlands government, having been asked to collaborate with Canadian economists at the University of Victoria to finish the analysis of his Balkans project.

A week later he put in writing:

> I will have finished most of my assignment here on Sunday. Do not know where you will be then. Please keep me up-to-date about whatever unfolds at your end. I am very serious about committing myself to you.

And then this empathetic message arrived from GJ on Facebook the next day:

> Just talked to somebody in NL [The Netherlands] on the phone about a totally unrelated subject. But suddenly realized how mentally and physically exhausting the past few weeks must have been for you. Please let me give you some peace in the coming months.

Here, I have to tell you straight up about one of our first conversations after he delivered himself back to my Vancouver world, so you'll know that I wasn't just free-falling and expecting love on a silver platter. GJ and I had been out for a dazzling walk on the beach and, as we headed for the stone steps back to the street, I inserted the key into the thoughts that had been bugging me about him.

"I broke it off with you last year because I thought you were a player, you know, and now I'm unclear about your relationship with Marie." I looked sideways at his profile and paused for his reaction. He took my hand.

We kept walking while he laughed and shook his head gently, saying that his life had mostly been consumed with his reports and work, which had often taken him to the University of Victoria. He did not 'do' the woman scene—or Marie, who was purely a colleague and a friend—but he had been thinking frequently of me and Nat over the course of the last year. With that, he squeezed my hand.

From that discussion onwards, we talked liberally about Nat's health hell and his summary report for his Balkans project, which used a community-development model to help the citizens heal from their post-traumatic stresses. We also celebrated how the world's focus was on Vancouver.

The earth was moving under my feet once more and we became lovers again, taking each day one at a time. Laughter was deposited again into my life, as well as non-prescribed activities. We managed to relax together and watch the full opening ceremony of the 2010 Winter Olympic Games, which was a great diversion from what felt like my rat maze. The entire city of Vancouver was abuzz, and Canadians were animated and energized by the extravaganza. For an evening, I honestly forgot that I was ill and that Nat was failing.

My man friend, Richard, had cautioned me to keep my health crisis under wraps, thinking that GJ would take off like a downhill ski racer. On the other hand, my cousin Evangeline (also known as Ev), my voice of reason, said, "You must tell him." So, after watching the opening show of the Winter Olympics and deciding that we had to walk through the downtown festivities at some point in the next few days, I put him into the picture of my situation.

I was sitting sideways on the couch with my feet up and wedged a bit under his right leg. With my fingers fluttering on my chin, I softly disclosed, "My cancer has come back, too. I just forget because I feel so well." GJ looked at me with soft eyes, took my hand and answered, "It doesn't matter. We'll look after it." And then I forgot about it again.

The following weeks seemed like clear sailing for him, while I was gripping the rudder tensely, as a mother and caretaker and—I almost forgot—a patient. The next month with Nat was all a blur. I merged with the family while our beautiful Nathalie slowly lost her body to that grotesque lottery called cancer thirteen days after her birthday. Her spirit remained strong until the pain-killing drugs fogged her brain. And, in spite of everything, Nat had more grace than I had ever witnessed in anyone in my life. I desperately wanted a miracle, but we all knew that it was what it was.

My daughter slid away to her playhouse in a parallel dimension just a month after the Vancouver Olympics and a part of me died with her. I was numb and exhausted and filled with images of her eyes during her last 'I love yous'. GJ was a solid companion and walked with me on the afternoon of her passing. He became an aide for all my immediate family and friends, claiming to understand loss from losing his parents and from the tragic demise of his fiancée, and he was considerately available to listen to any of us. And he was a great storyteller, taking us away from our lamenting numbness.

He moved in with me just before Nat's Celebration of Life, because of some tension that had been growing between him and Marie. When I picked him up from their condo, he had boxed and packed up all his things and was in a sweat to leave in a hurry, supposedly before she returned and met me and created a fracas.

It took some prodding, however, to get him to unpack and eventually bring his boxes in from the garage. He seemed to have an internal battle waging in his mind, which led me to think that he was a caring man, not wishing to hurt Marie too much. Under a sliver of a moon that evening, he proclaimed that there would be no more Vancouver Island trips because his work was wrapped up and he was free. His magic words were "And now I stay to take care of you." I remember so clearly tossing him my apprehension while sitting in the living room. I recapped that I was very vulnerable and that if the Marie thing was unresolved, he needed to return to her. He swore, over and over, that he was in love with me and glad to be by my side during the difficult recovery I was facing. He said that we were partners and would deal with the tough stuff together.

It was a happy/sad time in my life, but everyone saw GJ as my guardian angel. And indeed, GJ was a buffer for the first few months. If neighbours asked about Nat, he would squeeze my arm and gently shake his head, letting them know that I was fragile. Out in the community, if anyone mentioned their children, or activities that Nat had loved, or when I heard music that triggered me, he would kindly steer me in another direction or give me a little hug and hold my hand. His soul seemed to be available for mine to clutch like a stuffed animal.

I have to give him brownie points for being a helpful housemate as well. He emptied the dishwasher frequently, he helped spray-wash the patio, he replaced a signal light in my car and washed Bullwinkle sporadically, he rescued me from spiders and he once climbed up a borrowed ladder to retrieve my kitty, which had treed itself. He even vacuumed on occasion . . . and he could make me laugh!

So my point is that even though he turned out to be a disturbed and broken man, he was helpful and fun and did about as much housework as your average Canadian husband. So there were no red flags waving at the start.

At home, GJ listened attentively for my little inhalations that meant I'd come across something of Nat's. That blessed Dutchman also revealed his own anguish about nonsensical death, in tears one evening, broken up by deep sobs. A part of him still lamented Caroline, his betrothed, who had died in a car crash. So, he too understood sorrow. I ended up consoling him for his first true love and how he had never totally accepted its loss. We had grief as one of our common bonds.

He filled a part of the space left by Nat and a place in my heart that had been vacant for a year.

4

Excess Baggage

The heart has its reasons which reason knows nothing of.
— Blaise Pascal —

After just a few months of bumping into each other in my head and my home space, I whispered to my cousin Ev, my best and lifelong friend, the truth that my relationship with GJ had started to detour south. Of course, I defensively added that grief can dent any partnership. The reality was that practically living in each others' armpits had condensed its negative effects on a number of fronts.

To begin with, the honeymoon period was losing its romance. GJ would forget for long periods to say "I love you" and then, like a lightning bolt had hit, he would almost 'snap to' and apologize for neglecting to tell me how special I was. He was on-again, off-again like a light switch in his connection with me, not neglectful but certainly less and less available. His head was often elsewhere, but so was mine, so it wasn't a huge issue that we had passed the blissful beginning of our partnership and forgot to focus our attention on each other.

What GJ didn't forget was his history with women. Maybe just for something completely different, no matter what we were doing, he regularly mused over his lost fiancée (at least, too often for my well-being).

The juxtaposition of my suffering as a mother and his for his fiancée was confusing. After all, it had been thirty-something years since his bereavement, yet it seemed as fresh as yesterday to him.

Nevertheless, whether I wanted to attend or not, he additionally held seminars on the subject of his lost lovers, perhaps because he had met three of mine at Nat's Celebration of Life.

His first lecture, *Vrouwen* 101, happened just weeks after Nat's passing, when I had taken us out for a sushi lunch. At first, I thought that he was steering the conversation away from the fragile topics of motherhood, health and sadness but, out of left field, in the midst of the Japanese décor while I sipped my steaming miso soup, I got to know about the women.

Initially, it was an interesting distraction as GJ drifted to his most recent partner, Jana. However, my love of jasmine tea drifted somewhat that day, too. For some reason, he felt the need to tell me everything about her. As left-handed GJ dipped into his tempura sauce without dripping on himself, he put her in the picture as the one he'd left before he came to Canada as Marie's Ph.D advisor.

He had loved the beautiful and much younger Portuguese poet, known in her country simply as Jana. They had met through a male cousin of hers, who had befriended GJ when walking the Way of St. James in Spain. They hit it off so well that GJ followed him to his hometown, Braga, in northwestern Portugal, where he and Jana were introduced.

They fell in love quickly because she was magnificent and very talented and, although he didn't say this part, I assumed that he was fascinating and very alluring to her in turn. Jana parented two young children and soon begged him to share her spectacular home in Braga and her ancestral vacation home in Sarajevo. They appreciated each other, as GJ put it, for a tumultuous but passionate couple of years.

Jana was a firecracker with her children, her poetry and especially with him, but he loved that about her. She was the boss, a force to be reckoned with. She occasionally still contacted him, although he respectfully did

Excess Baggage

not elaborate again on that. He just said that she wanted him back, and that was uncomfortable for him. While I wondered about the money that he said she had been asking him for around the time of our breakup, it just didn't feel like a critical time to bite on those old details.

I'm Canadian, so I'm nice, but that felt like one of the longest lunches of my adult life. I listened to him go back in time, having an inner banquet of memory stew. GJ then decided to pencil in facts about the gorgeous Dutch woman Barbra, who had owned his heart for a period of time before Jana and who owned her own boutique hotel near Hamburg, Germany, where they'd lived a life of luxury. Barbra was also a skier, a tennis player and a cyclist. He initially won her over with his athleticism, but that union struggled through an on-again, off-again relationship for five years. GJ said heartlessly that she was obsessed with her looks (which he claimed were exceptional), her hotel, her sports and her borzoi dog. He said it had been hard to find where he fit in.

By the time I was stuffing the last of my smoked salmon maki rolls into my expanding stomach, he told me—with that twinkly eye thing that he does—about the woman I reminded him of. That was Annelies, a Dutch doctor whom he said he had met when his sons played in a soccer league with her son. They had taken it slowly so that the children could be comfortable with their 'putting the dots on the i's', as the Dutch would say, before they moved in together. GJ shared a home with Annelies and her son and daughter for ten years in Belgium and his sons visited frequently. Life was easy with her, and she had been his favourite.

What he told me could have been embellished. I'm just recounting it as simply as I can. GJ cooed that Annelies was intelligent, beautiful—I dare to share that he also said sensual and compassionate—and a great step-mom for his sons. On the other hand, she had a daughter with an eating disorder and that was what stressed the relationship to the point of no return.

She has married since he left her and now has another son from that union, but GJ repeatedly claimed that he blew it when he took the easy

Walking on Heads

way out by grabbing for the younger, childless Barbra. In reflection, GJ admitted that Barbra had merely been a mid-life fling and a big mistake. Annelies was the one he wished he'd been more patient with. GJ went on and on, until I wondered if he was ever going to run out of breath. I hadn't even had a chance to put an end to a single one of his sentences when—in full view of the other diners—he said candidly that he wished he had settled down and married her. I imagine that I was supposed to think that we might marry one day, but my truth was that, even though I'd wanted more from Jack, I sincerely had no interest in saying "I do" with him and putting my daughter's inheritance at risk.

Finally, GJ paused as if to take an intermission. My mouth was again full, so he carried on to blow off the woman he rarely talked about (but who was of most interest to me). That was Anne, his ex-wife and the mother of his children. All GJ would say was that Anne had been a women's libber, a horse lover and a cabaret performer, and that she had run off with another man while still pregnant with his twin boys. I actually scratched my head as a part of me wondered about her side of the story and why GJ rarely mentioned his sons, Daniel and Michiel, except to declare that he had dependably paid child support. It was like pulling teeth to get him to say much about them, apart from that they were both athletic and intellectual like him, which caused some competitive stress between father and sons at times.

I think that he was trying to assure me that he was not a player by revealing his past relationships. I had my three significant men, he had his four or five women. I lost count. I also believe that his intention was to make me comfortable with the European women who were in his head with us at our table. He didn't brag, just filled in the blanks he assumed I needed to know about.

While I kept my game face on, GJ next handed me the 'goods' on Caroline. Many of us think we have a touching first love story, but GJ's was to die for, as the absurd saying goes. It was genuinely catastrophic, but I thought that I had already heard enough about his sorrow and the pedestal that Caroline had been put on. Nevertheless, GJ told me more, even though I was desperate at that point to get the bill and leave. At the same time, I had an overwhelming nosiness about this contestant who held his heart in limbo.

Despite his sapphire-blue eyes, the room grew dark with his memories. Every summer, GJ and his family would meet up with GJ's father's best friend Karl and his Swiss family. They would hike and rock-climb as well as go boating, swimming and cycling. The families were both supremely athletic. One summer, Caroline suddenly grew up in GJ's eyes and the two fell in big love (as the Dutchman would say)!

Unfortunately, GJ tastelessly introduced this visual in view of the other patrons, with tears wetting his eyes: Caroline had been driving from school in Paris to her home in Switzerland when her car left the road. She would have been the same age as Nathalie, but Caroline was a victim of driver fatigue. GJ was devastated by her loss. I scrounged through my mind to find some sense or direction in the mixed bag of my thoughts on this tragedy.

He muttered that her memory messed him up and he still had a hard time dealing with her death. Then he seemed to come out of his trance and whispered, "Am I in total disgrace for dominating this lunch?"

I could only look compassionately at his upset face and fib, "It's okay. Now I appreciate more of what I need to know about you."

It seemed to me that no woman had yet compared to his inner narrative about that last goddess, and that maybe that was why he claimed he could not settle down. My feelings were that all of his women may have experienced a thinly-veiled devaluation in comparison to his high esteem of this Caroline, and that the soft challenge for each of us was to trump her memory and heal him.

After the lunch and a leisurely walk along the waterfront at what's known to locals as Kits Beach, with a direct view of Stanley Park on the right and a swath of other beaches on the left all the way out to the University of British Columbia, GJ expressed his delight: "What a

walking on Heads

weather!" As spring was strutting its magnificence in the cherry blossoms and in the sweet zephyrs fanning the water, I realized how, again and again, GJ could be set off recalling the Swiss Miss whenever I mentioned Nathalie. His chronicles highlighted to me how grief can be like a poison if it is not eventually put to rest.

GJ's reflections on the other women, especially Caroline, were repeatedly curdling my stomach, warping my mind and heart and denting our sex life. I had heard too often about them all, especially the elusive memory of the gilded girl.

On top of that, I was flummoxed by how he hardly left the house to work, childishly parked his inactive cellphone in the front hall on the floral table and didn't have any money. My brain waves returned to his lack of cash, or what may have been stinginess. Did he lose his generosity when he lost Caroline? Who doesn't carry loose change in a pocket or two? And I suspected that he might have been as tight-fisted with the truth about himself as he was with his money—which, come to think of it, were one and the same. I considered that corner of my mind that houses the unspeakable and wondered if his flaw was that he was a cheap bastard in more ways than was obvious.

5

Sitting on Black Seed

*An excuse is worse than a lie,
for an excuse is a lie, guarded.*

— Alexander Pope —

The money buzz was that GJ had left Marie—his Canadian roommate and student—in a bit of a rush, because it turns out she was in love with him and they were not seeing eye-to-eye on that front. To him, they were only in an intellectual relationship and the pressure to feel more had become too onerous. The poor guy (pardon the double entendre) had walked out on her in a flurry of high drama, leaving his wallet and sunglasses in the glove compartment of her car. He went straight from her home to mine . . . and from her pocket to mine, as it turns out.

It was a very kind and convincing performance he put on when he took my face into his large hands and tenderly said to me, "This is a delicate situation. Marie is very angry and vulnerable owing to our work relationship and my abrupt departure. We had both seen this end coming but she's felt abandoned before and I don't want to remind her about that day. She's mad, sad and embarrassed. I need to give her some cooling-down time. And my dear, it would be better if she didn't know about my feelings for you yet. That would be too messy."

Call me innocent! I of course understood, from one woman's heart to

Walking on Heads

another. Plus, given my grief and the 'overwhelm' of my own life—and the fact that Etta was singing "At Last" in the other room at the time—I didn't question that fiction until my emotional turmoil and dense sense of loss had settled down a few degrees.

A couple of months later, however, GJ was still separated from his wallet, credit cards and even the loose loonies or toonies that everyone finds in their pockets, even on the sidewalk. Still, through some twisted logic, he did have his passport and driver's papers.

Sometimes I thought that our little misunderstandings about this subject were swirling between us because of the cultural schism, or that I was confused by his translation of the account of his miracle passport and driver's licence, so I zoned out on his idiotic attempts at explanations. Despite the hole in his pocket, he was still a terrific roommate, challenging my funny bone at the right times, testing my intellect and being a kind caretaker of my heart.

I remember precisely the moment I broke the silence about his missing wallet, or at least its contents. It was raining, so I knew he couldn't take off on his bicycle . . . or head back to the computer, because it was doing its backup. So I mentioned the wallet.

I was hoping and praying that Marie had told him she had made his bank cards available for pickup or maybe, just maybe, my anticipation was hungry for the news that he had made arrangements to replace the contents. So, with a little hiccup, I tottered into the conversation about it.

"Dutchman, will you be getting your wallet and cards back soon from Marie? We could pick them up from her. Or have you just cancelled the cards? It must be hard to be without spare change. And . . . who keeps their driver's licence separate from their money?" (Subtlety is not my strong suit sometimes.)

Well, annoyed doesn't begin to describe the flash of fury I felt from him, which instantly changed to irritation and then morphed into that twinkling-eyes thing that gets me every time.

I could practically hear crickets, as he took his time grinding out a deadpan answer. "My dear, it's a European habit. We keep our driver's

Sitting on Black Seed

card and passports in our travelling pockets. And about my debit and credit cards . . . it's okay, I'm taking care of it!"

These were words that I would hear over and over and over... echoing, like the Dutch phrase *op zwart zaad zitten* (sitting on black seed), which, incidentally, means being penniless or barren or unproductive. Black seeds are infertile, space-squatters that have no potential or value.

The monetary conversation was in dire need of being on a marquee, but by chance, on that very evening I was pouting about the cash flow, we rented the film *The Girl with the Dragon Tattoo*. It had an intelligent plot, but the rape scenes were too violent and uncomfortable for me, so we debriefed on it as we were slipping into bed. Shockingly, GJ's main comment was that the stunning young lead actress reminded him of his Caroline!

My choked reaction was to wonder if she had been raped and by whom but, instead, I just recalled that today his perfect Caroline would be his age—that is, over fifty—and not so spritely and smooth. I then lifted myself from the comfort of his body heat and showed him a pretty picture of me at the actress's age, one where I was in the doting and shielding arms of Paul (back when he was my boyfriend), but I'm not sure he got the point.

I bumped my way back to the money discussion the next evening, after my fur had smoothed down a bit. This included our first adopting-a-dog conversation. Part of that chat involved exploring his 'style' of pet parenting, his commitment to caring for an animal and his contribution financially, because I couldn't afford to support another body. GJ gave me the lowdown on the German Shepherd he had raised when the boys were young, and I liked how attentive he seemed and that his approach had in fact been more parental than domineering alpha male. He also agreed to pay for our dog and take it with him, should our canine outlive me.

Looking back, it seems illogical, but I cuddled the idea of a new life coming into the house. The joint plan to rescue an animal from a shelter was a bonding, reassuring gesture, saying that he was in the game with me. Also, it gave me something new to mother.

Walking on Heads

My innards were settling down and summer was in the air, I thought. It looked like I would keep shelling out for things for the time being, including the dog, and then we could split up our costs after his finances were settled. Hiding the fact that when we double-dated he never, ever, sprang for the bill was getting awkward. It was embarrassing, so I avoided going out, using the not-untrue excuse that I was still socially fragile from dealing with the drama and aftermath of Nat's death.

When we went food shopping, he would come along, push the cart and then carry the groceries. I had never had a man leap to grocery shop with me before! Still, during the swiping of the cards, he was always looking elsewhere or chatting with someone and working the room. For that reason, he had no idea about the high price of food in my part of the world as compared to the Netherlands. He seemed to assume that because gas prices were lower, food and dining costs would be the same. As if!

Consequently, we had fewer and fewer lunch 'dates' that I would pay for. I was begrudging him his laissez-faire attitude and wondering where the term 'going Dutch' came from as I was sorting through a variety of unfamiliar judgments and opinions about him being a kept man.

GJ was 'working' from my home office every day and occupying my computer for hours a day, despite the gorgeous weather. He let me know that he was doing research and outreach on the internet, planning his next proposal for his Ministry, and the long list of bookmarks seemed to support that. I had gone a little deaf on that topic at times. I just hoped that he was taking care of the lost credit and debit cards—and his laptop, which still lived with Marie for some reason.

The next time that I dared to prod him about his economic situation was a Tuesday afternoon in early May, after having a snooze in Nat's old bedroom. Before the respite, I had been poring over my bills and sweating. I was genuinely concerned about my small disability income and the cash-flow problem, and I was on pins and needles as to how GJ would respond to the topic.

Sitting on Black Seed

As I gazed onto his face with its perfect nose, it registered for the first time that his eyes were often bloodshot from his contact lenses and that he had nose hairs. Rather longish ones, too. The handsomeness of the Dutchman was disappearing as fast as his excuses were emerging.

"Umm, Dutchman, I, umm, (deep inhale) . . . Vancouver has one of the highest costs of living in the world. Look, I am embarrassed that I should be so jumbled about my money, but I'm on a disability pension as well as still paying back the loan I took out to renovate the house. Will you, umm, have money to contribute . . . soon?" The tone of my voice was that of a nice Canadian woman, a little apologetic for bothering him.

Looking into that handsome yet annoyed face offered me a new view of GJ. I either had a déjà vu experience or a psychic one as I predicted what his swatting-at-a-fly response would sound like. He could hardly look me in the eyes as he quickly answered, as if he was ranting about an exasperating politician, "I've taken care of it. Don't worry, the Ministry's accountant is dealing with it and we should be okay in a couple of weeks."

Well, knock me over with a feather!

The fog of my trauma over losing my child and dealing with that ghastly aftermath was replaced by the strain of being confused week after week by assurances that his wallet and cards would resurface. I felt like my interior was being squeezed in a vise, smothering my famous sensitivity. I felt so very lonely because I couldn't talk to anyone about it yet, except for sharing snippets with my cousin Ev and my friends Nicole and Bryn, who had guessed something was grating at me. To the rest of the world, I bandaged the truth with my smile.

I figured the time had come to look for our dog. It filled some awkward hours as we checked out the available canines in our area, reading up about them and agreeing on the size of dog that we could manage. He wanted a big bruiser and I wanted a medium-sized mutt, but in the end, neither of us had the upper hand regarding size.

It was heartbreaking how many dogs in animal shelters had been abused or abandoned, and how they had from mild to severe behaviour problems from heartless mistreatment. I didn't have the physical or emotional energy to re-school a scarred dog, although a part of me wanted to save one.

It was clear that I had always been a caretaker and an INFP (introverted, intuitive, feeling, perceptive) type according to a Myers-Briggs personality type team-building exercise I had done with at a professional development day with the school district. This means that I am calm and deal with things according to how I feel about them. I am an idealist, I'm highly intuitive and flexible, and I am sensory versus being crazy about dealing with things logically. Maybe getting a dog wasn't logical, but it was a compassionate choice.

Since Nat's loss, I think I pined to select a new body to tutor and save from harm. I longed for a cause. However, when we visited a couple of shelters, our dog chose us. She was louder than the rest, which got GJ's attention, and she wagged her tail more furiously than any of the others, which got mine. And she was a sweetheart.

However, she had big paws and I could see that she might still be growing. I wanted a smaller version of the sweet, happy creature, but GJ convinced me that she was the one. And she was! She had been a stray and had only been staying at the SPCA for a few weeks and, given her kind nature, we knew she would be adopted if we didn't make our move. We took her for a walk a couple of times while discussing the imminent joys of welcoming a new warm body into the family.

Dona merged with our household and became at one with the lawn and the backyard in the early summer and, although my garden will never be quite the same (nor the lawn), I love her. GJ was the main walker because I tired easily from the cumulative effects of my oral chemo pills and because it was frankly nice to get him out of the house a couple of times a day.

Having our sweet Dona join us helped me cope with my grief by focusing on the upside of things and allowing my sense of humour to return, as Nat would have wanted. There were four little maids in my world again. I conceed that GJ was very compassionate with the dog

Sitting on Black Seed

and cat, with my friends, my neighbours' children, my daughter, my ex, my grief, and on and on. He was upbeat, happy to be on the beautiful west coast, pleased with me and busy doing remote business from my computer . . . or so I thought.

He gently held the space whenever Maxine came over to help me go through Nat's things or simply talk. He was very attentive, sympathetic and unselfish about us sharing time as part of our recovery. He waited on us like we were royalty, and he gave us room to reminisce. He even suggested that we take a week and 'do' San Francisco . . . which we did, as a gift from my father. GJ happily took care of Dona and the kitty while we were away.

Too good to be true was what I sometimes thought for the first few months. It felt like the sun was always shining, and so what? On the one hand, he was gentle and caring about my sadness and accompanied me to several of my medical appointments and treatments. Combined with all this consideration and his solicitous actions, I can add that he hardly ever burped, never mind belched. He did not snore or keep me awake at night, and I swear that I heard fewer musical tunes from his intestines than from my past lovers. On the other hand, he could be a very sloppy housemate, he was a fast eater, he left beard shavings in my bathroom sink and where did those fatty bags under his eyes come from? In many ways he was a girl's superlative partner, except for the money thing and the illusive work days.

So I no longer worried about him being too magnificent to be real. I made hay while the sun was shining and I parked the money problem for a while longer.

However, one overcast morning a few weeks after my chat-with-self about his perfect little imperfections, I returned early from a visit with my cousin because of a migraine to find GJ on the phone with Marie. I knew that she had called before, but I wondered if he was also calling her.

"How's Marie doing?" Luckily, I don't have a jealous gene in me, so my question was benign and innocent.

Walking on Heads

"She's having some dilemmas about whether to work on another research project or to accept a term position at Ryerson University in Toronto. So, she called for my advice."

"It sounded like you were arguing . . .," I ventured, sensing that they had benefited from several furtive conferences. For a moment, the silence hovered like a foul smell, as if Dona had broken wind.

"No, she's just annoyed that I can't help her to make up her mind. And she was wondering if I could ask my funders in Europe to support a second part of her project in the Balkans, but I'm telling her it's a conflict of interest." There was a pause, then GJ softly muttered, "I'm afraid that she will follow me to Zanzibar, wanting to work together again . . ." Then he gave me a hug and a sweet kiss on each fingertip.

The next morning, after my bath, I thought that the house was empty and I figured that GJ had taken Dona for a walk in the fog, or that he was off to play tennis at the indoor courts. The computer was on, so I assumed that he would be back soon. I checked into Facebook and scanned his photos list, finding one of him standing on a beach with his arms wrapped around a short, slightly-older woman who looked like the Marie I had seen him clutching like a little boy a few months ago on Fourth Avenue. As I lifted my head from the computer to squint at Dona in the garden, I caught sight of GJ sitting on the bench. It looked like he was on the phone, again arguing with someone.

Downstairs, the TV was also on (to a rerun of *Desperate Housewives*, of all things) and, in front of me, his e-mail screen was open. He hadn't logged out of his account. I didn't figure he'd be outside for long, so despite a sudden crazy headache, I did something I had never done ever in my life: I checked someone else's e-mail messages.

There in front of my kaleidoscope eyes, at the top of the page, rested a note sent off an hour before to a 'Jana', who I supposed was the Portuguese lover from his past. Just before that bombshell, my eyes zeroed in on a message to Marie. I zipped straight to that one because her header read, "Back from Far and Away". I didn't snatch the chance to read the

Sitting on Black Seed

message to Jana. My lightning choice was to peek more into the note to Marie, hoping and praying that there finally would be a clue about his wallet.

Anyhow, the e-mail reply to Marie went drastically beyond an answer to a request for his property. I found she didn't even mention the wallet or sunglasses or his laptop, as I strained my aching eyes for details. The conversation may have had some items about her Balkan research, but just as the back door banged open I thought I might have seen the word 'herpes'. I instantly closed the message and scooted into the washroom to flush the toilet to cover the sounds of my cursing.

From that afternoon onward, I took delivery of a collection of more and more headaches. Despite weekly massages, my smothered subconscious seemed to be sending me memos that I was not picking up on yet. I was drained from trying to figure out what else was decomposing for me about GJ. I became conscious that the fellow sometimes spoke gibberish and that he was demonstrably less affectionate. Crowning that, thrusting into my little head was the fact that he still lacked even an iota of cash. Whenever I started to ask, as in "Look, GJ, isn't it time for us to go on a date—you know the kind where you take me out and you pay?" or "Have many people told you about the odd way you sometimes describe things?", something inside said, *Don't press it, Anni*. So I started to hold back from him, all the while counterfeiting a blissful facade for my friends and family while my insides twisted with uncertainty and turmoil.

6
When the Horse is Dead, Get Off!

> *Beat me with the truth, don't torture me with lies.*
>
> — Unknown —

It was crazy-making to feel so alone in my dilemma, yet so crowded by this guy who hardly seemed to work anywhere but at my desk and in front of my computer. I became moody and I couldn't even describe the issues to my close friends or my children's dad, because it was hard to explain and awkward to admit that the man of my dreams was a deadbeat.

This cooling off towards him wasn't monthly mood stuff, but a depression expanding exponentially alongside the effects of the IV chemo I was now receiving. I didn't really understand why I was so distressed, except that I wanted my space back, as well as the GJ I fell in love with.

It seemed that he was constantly ranting about the Dutch elections and the xenophobic voters in the Netherlands. For weeks, he had been bewildered by the Dutch having become anti-Muslim and scared of their shadows (according to him). He was angry with the government that employed him and was thinking of retiring, and he also fumed about changing his citizenship. His father had been German and he was seriously thinking of applying to become German himself.

Walking on Heads

Was it a coincidence, then, that GJ asked me to help him to look for a waterfront acreage near Vancouver Island to buy as his retirement investment? Believe me, it seemed like a bonding thing to do, so—indulgent Anni that I am—I exclaimed, "Sweet! That could be fun, and an important asset for your winding-down years." We did hours of research and connected with a realtor on Saturna Island, which is the southeasternmost of the Gulf Islands chain off the British Columbian coast. GJ looked forward to taking me there for a week-long vacation in October, after the tourist season.

My advisors, Ev and Bryn, asked me several times, as if they had rehearsed their questions, "Are you thinking of mortgaging or selling your house and being part of the Saturna deal?" Each time, I succinctly and truthfully answered that I would not contribute to GJ's venture. We all silently understood that I would not gamble Maxine's inheritance, but instead give GJ's property idea wholly over to his dreams of being a mini-land baron. Besides, he never asked me to liquidate my assets, nor did he ever open up a Canadian bank account.

Sound the heraldry horns, because around that same time period—actually, within two weeks of the investment idea—GJ staged a big production, like a Shakespearean tragedy. He announced that he had been directed to return to the Hague to report to his Ministry and give a keynote address at their AGM.

I remember that it was a Monday. His soliloquy was apologetic: with dramatic melancholy in his sapphire eyes, he pronounced that he would have to leave hastily for a couple of weeks. GJ declared that there was some political foofaraw regarding the Dutch election and the forming of the new coalition government, which had been in limbo for months. He wasn't quite sure when the Ministry was having its emergency confab, but he would know soon . . . within a day. And he wanted to be home to observe and listen to the people's opinions on the wild Wilders gentleman who looked like a modern man but spoke like a medieval tyrant.

So (drum roll) here is the defining moment, when I snagged my soul on the biggest barnacle on the beach. The next morning, after we

When the Horse is Dead, Get off!

had immersed ourselves in a west coast breakfast of fruit salad, yoghurt and muffins with almond butter out on the garden patio, GJ said that he had just been given the directive to make tracks back to the Hague on Thursday. While I had been showering, he had made arrangements for his new credit and debit cards to be available for signing while he was in Holland. He said that he had put pressure on his accountant to wrap things up and prepare to transfer some of his Greek bonds to a savings account at a Canadian bank so that he could buy property here.

I was twitching over the Greek part and started to blurt, "Who would buy your bonds and are they worth much?" but I stopped myself as he lay those soft, beautiful lips on mine, captured my hand and led me into the house, where I forgot what I was asking.

Now, this is the part that even I don't wholly get. Perhaps if my confidante Ev hadn't been away in the Caribbean, she might have uttered a warning about how brainless it was, but it was what it was. GJ hinted that he needed a loan to pay for his flight and for travel pocket change. In a bit of a sweat (not from the bed Olympics, but because of my small savings account), I worried—yes, worried—that he might lose his job if someone found out that he'd lost his cards and couldn't get back to home base. Thinking back, he never actually suggested that his honour or career were at stake, but I, not he, agonized over it. Maybe it was because I was not able to fix Nat when she was so ill—that would explain my need to serve and protect my partner from my own appraisal of the complications his wooden shoes might snag on.

There you have it: whether I went up the ladder or down, my position was shaky. Wednesday evening, after a fabulous dinner cooked by Maxine, I lay in his arms in bed. I could hear the thudding of his heart as he gently lifted me off his right shoulder and brought my chin to his face. "I don't have to go tomorrow if you want me to stay."

What would you have done? Really, at this point I know, I know, I really know that there were several options, but the one I saw was crystal clear and I'll never know what might have happened if I had chosen a different answer. My simple reply was that he had to give his keynote. He was up against a new government, which preferred to put their funds into their military and East African endeavours and they needed his propositions and analyses and goals to support their local governance.

So I lent GJ $1400.00 in tax-free Canadian cash and expected him 'home' in three weeks, at the most. After a very passionate kiss, he shed bluish tears at the airport and flung me another kiss as he walked away, pulling his bags behind him and soulfully looking back over his right shoulder at me.

7

A Woman Scorned is Like a Rodeo Clown

Words are cheap. The biggest thing you can say is 'elephant.'
— Charlie Chaplin —

Now in the Hague, preparing for presentation tomorrow. Up till now it has been an interesting rollercoaster ride with more setbacks! I am happy you are doing fine! I have lots to tell you, but must find the appropriate time. After the presentation and a few other meetings on Wednesday there is some breathing space!

Love you, my sweetie! Say hello to everyone!
GJ

    I buried my face in my pillow quite a few times during that period, given that a month after this note, GJ's homecoming was yet again delayed. He had been e-mailing me about all of the barriers he was facing and the extra commitments he had with his work, and I still had not had my money returned. His explanation was that the Netherlands government had sent him first to Paris and then to Vienna to handle some negotiations regarding funding for his new proposed project in

Walking on Heads

Zanzibar. And, of course, next he would be sent to Dar es Salaam to do some exploration of Tanzania's developmental aid needs.

> Getting homesick. Guess you are having your chemo right now. Can see you out there in Vancouver, probably Bryn is with you now. Here it is a circus, but because I sort of delivered an inspired, maybe provocative speech, my concept is getting more interest. I will be on a plane to Paris when you get out of the chemo. I have some meetings at UNESCO Paris. Seems promising. Anyway: I feel I embarked on a rocky journey! I hope Dona behaves while I am away.
>
> Gosh, I hope I soon get into some more quiet times, so as to communicate with the far away west coast and . . . finally return to you. That coast is such a paradise from my (now European) perspective. The Saturna realty search is still on! After the weekend I will have some time to reconnect on that issue too. Hey lover, keep the spirits up. I bloody miss you, but I am sure you are having all the right support from Maxine and all those lovely friends.
>
> Big hugs,
> GJ

A few days later, sitting on his wall on Facebook, GJ had a new post typed up and attached to some YouTube music:

> The summer of 1982 was the best of my life. I spent every loving moment with the most beautiful, smart and entrancing woman I have ever or will ever know.

A Woman Scorned is Like a Rodeo Clown

I assumed he had visited Caroline's crash site and was in mourning . . . again. Still, this bizarre declaration made me feel a little invisible, especially considering that he had befriended thirteen of my friends and family on Facebook and that they might wonder (along with me), what the heck? I let it go and got on with showing my happy face to Maxine that evening as we took in a movie together.

However, about a week later, after I had dashed through a haze of flying midges on my way to the house from the garage, I opted to sit and have a mug of hot chocolate and relax my body. I still had unexpected flashbacks and moments of labyrinthine sadness. Sometimes I would go with it and talk out loud to Nathalie, and frequently I would just wail and bawl for a while, missing her laughter, her wisdom, her smells and just . . . her. This time, I blubbered and sniffed, thinking it should have been me to die first.

Although I was sipping at the now-cool decadent liquid, I decided to change the subject in my head and my heart by checking my e-mail, hoping for a response from my stepdaughters, Michelle and Sophia, who had been invited to dine with Maxine, Liana, their mom, Marcia, and myself on the weekend.

Lo and behold, my man had resurfaced.

> Hi my sweetheart,
>
> I am still in Vienna, working on a joint proposal with the OPEC Fund for Zanzibar. I am so immersed in the work that I often forget there is a home front too. I read your last e-mail and I am happy you can manage with our lovely Dona. Is she still trying to dig her way next door? Congrats for Maxine's birthday: I hope she and Liana spent the day in good spirits. Is the chemo still having only relatively mild effects? Be sure, I want to wrap this up here sooner than later: the peace and quiet of the west coast is dearly missed! And really looking forward

to our morning coffees in the garden and (of course!), the walks with Dona. And boy, I unfortunately am now totally behind in the Doc Martin saga, too.

Maybe I can be back before your birthday, but I am far from certain yet, as still many obstacles need to be cleared here (and in wretched Holland). I keep you posted on that. Conrad sent me a message on the property we were interested in. Please inform him that I will take care of that upon returning home, because my life here in Vienna is a bit too chaotic to also take on the administrative procedures of investing in property. Will call when I land in Dar.

Big hugs and many kisses,
GJ

Like a rodeo clown in the saddle, my bank balance—as well as my emotional balance—was fluctuating. I come from a school which values having a beginning, a middle and an end to things, and I wanted the money crisis to be finished. All the while, GJ continued with the same blank tape whenever I (creatively, with the most mental agility I could muster) asked for money:

"GJ, the cat is meowzling for food and climbing the walls, and Dona needs bones" ... "Dr. Jank, I'm behind in my payments for meditation classes and you like that pretzel thing that I do with my legs" ... "I need a haircut since my fringe is infringing on my eyesight."

In each case, the remarks he repeatedly replied with were just these:

Anni, my sweetie, Indeed, sorry. The 'fatherland' is demanding some answers. :-(I will take care of things when I come back to your delightful embrace.

A Woman Scorned is Like a Rodeo Clown

I do not consider patience a virtue. I think that it can sometimes, especially in cases like this, be an impediment to presenting the truth. *No news is the news*, is what my little voice kept chirping. *He cannot possibly give a damn if he keeps flipping off your financial SOS.* I was also thinking that loyalty, truth and charity are up for interpretation. What I did learn was that there are some people who count on the rest of us being honest, sincere, faithful and principled.

At this point, I was getting the scent that his story about his job might be legitimate, but his lack of integrity about the money he owed me stunk like an elephant in the room. The money excuses were not only annoying, but also made me queasy when I thought of how I had stood by my man and given him the benefit of the doubt. He had seemed like a decent, solid man, but his lack of respect for my situation was debilitating.

The most difficult part was the isolation I felt from not knowing what was really happening. Yet, remembering his bloodshot eyes and all the wine and beer) he had enjoyed when he stayed with me, I started to wonder whether I honestly wanted him back. Still, I tried another light-hearted e-mail.

l(a

le
af
fa
ll

s)
one
l

iness ... Like e.e. cummings, I am feeling out of sight, out of mind and out of order. Although it would be nice if you would call, or better still, arrive home soon, I need something else even more... something that no doubt has not even been in your daily consciousness (or conscience).

Please, *gelieve*, e-mail your banker to wire transfer funds to my bank account. I lent you $1400, bought the bicycle for you, paid for a couple of pricey phone calls to Holland and several to Ontario, covered the costs for Dona, and I will have to pay extra income tax for cashing in some of my Registered Retirement Savings bonds to pay for supporting an extra adult... so, a token for each month you stayed here would genuinely help.

Yes, I wish it was only me that's lonely, but the bank account is also drier than the falling hazelnut leaves on the garden patio.

Met liefde,
Anni

I was starting to formulate the theory that I had been in love with a mock-up of a gentleman, like a paper doll cut-out. The shining guy had dulled in my eyes and I was also realizing that he was not the 'real deal'. In fact, I was experiencing double vision from this whole mess.

When the next part of his story arrived, my friends scrunched their faces at me and used four-lettered words to describe his behaviour and his lack of principles. What set them off? Why was the Goddess of Thunder making a racket?

It was plain and simple: GJ never, ever phoned me from Europe or Africa. His excuses were that there was an enormous time contest between all his random meetings and travelling and report deadlines. Oh, and he also forgot my birthday!

I had stood by my man because it was beyond my comprehension, first of all, that this thoughtful guy might be lying to me or have a damaged personal truth. And second, how could he be callous, given what I had been through over the past year? I had cancer and, even though I didn't dwell on it, I couldn't imagine anyone taking advantage of that. He wouldn't possibly add to my emotional fragility as a mother, would he? And third, he said he loved me and still did . . . unless his English was off. Was he laughing at me behind my back for being so gullible and so uncharacteristically patient? I couldn't go there, because that would mean that I was ridiculous and foolish to have handed over all my trust to someone who was not worthy or respectable. Still, embarrassment hovered over me like a mosquito. As for his response to that last request for the money, GJ kept me on the hook:

> Extremely busy and very little access to phone or internet in Tanzania because of power rationing. You are NOT out of sight or out of mind. Back in Dar I will be able to contact you. And, indeed, it's high time to go home!
>
> Big hugs and kisses, my sweetie,
> your GJ

My friends were concerned that his attitude was too cavalier. In fact, Maxine, who does not mince words, even spewed out, "Hasn't he heard of a calling card or Skype, for fuck's sake?" GJ's travel story had become even more like a complex run-on sentence. I was curious, furious and sick from eating so much chocolate, which usually reminded me of times when all was well but was not working anymore.

Yet, I continued bravely on and sent him a short note to test the waters:

> Dear GJ,
>
> I hope that you have been healthy and safe, or at least are now. I expect that you are enormously busy, unlike

me who skiffs along a bit like Sisyphus. Patience has never been my strong suit so I'll be straightforward: come back to me is my request.

xo,
A

GJ obviously didn't recognize the quote from the story *Cold Mountain*, nor the irony in that I did not consider him to be in danger and we were not the loves of each other's lives, but when this e-mail turned up, I knew why I was still confused about his position. GJ wrote in mid-December:

Dearest Anni,

It is early morning here and I am off to the airport to fly back to Stone Town. Will finish status report to be sent to Dutch for comment. I must be on standby again for a couple of more days. Tedious and boring, but since I have committed myself to this project my orders are to wrap things up here. So, all this has nothing to do with my feelings for you or hesitations about our relationship.
I am just doing my job here and that takes all my energy. I will be glad when all this will be over and I have pulled through successfully. Indeed, I am forced to neglect other responsibilities but I hope I can make up for that later. :-(

Best wishes and lots of love,
your GJ

A Woman Scorned is Like a Rodeo Clown

PS. Indeed I need to contact Maxine, so I will as soon as I have the time. Please don't be angry with me for my briefness: this is all written in a hurry.

Kiss. Kiss. Kiss.

My answer:

(* ~ *) mwah.

His reply:

Have no idea what that means! I want to be old-fashioned and not get into that sort of texting or twitter language. Too hard to decipher. And indeed, I will say goodbye to Facebook soon too, as it has become a Goldman Sachs financial toy. Africa surely radicalizes a person!

Me, the next afternoon:

Go have a good sleep. (I was only sending you my own stylized smile from my phone because you will be back to celebrate your birthday with me!) I do not twitter or blog but might eventually to support Max's music or some engaging new project. But that remains to be.

Forgive me for seeming or being TOO western. I am feeling sensitive and confused by your harsh quip or maybe I should say your attitude about my artistic happy face yesterday. I do get that you were tired and possibly frustrated but I don't deserve to be snapped at. You do!

Walking on Heads

If you want to be an old-fashioned guy, it's not okay to hurt your woman's feelings. And an old-fashioned guy (from my recollection) would also do what he says he would do—such as phone his lady when he says he would and also settle up debts in a timely way. I loved your old-fashioned self who was my shield and who made me feel more important than adventures in Neverland.

So, to wrap up MY rant, remember that I am vulnerable and slowly ailing. You might even choose an old-fashioned relationship and trust your able colleague to do his job, and then you can return to me and Dona. Just come back so we can kiss and make up like Doc Martin and Louisa.

Night! Night!

His retort:

Sorry, my dear. I was indeed touchy and tired. Now off to Mozambique.

A person has to draw the line somewhere, and I did. I let him know, in written language, that his behaviour was clearly in the wrong. Now isn't 'sorry' a sapid word? (That's a cross between 'vapid' and 'sappy'.) As much as he was avoiding me and the west coast—and apparently my daughter, whom he never did write until February—his next miserable storyline, like water off a duck's back, was about another detour to Dodoma. It was hard to find my philosophical backbone. I know that this probably seems like such a weak yarn, but I was in for a penny, in for a pound, as they say. So, I persisted with the garbage e-mails longing for him to come back so I could slap and then shake and lastly thump him on his way out my back door.

A Woman Scorned is Like a Rodeo Clown

He had the audacity to write to me that he and his replacement were being asked to travel for East African Commission meetings again, on a weekend. At that point, already sensing his answer, as Dona ran to the back window with a bark aimed at a seagull that was trying to find cat or dog food crumbs in the yard, I reminded him on Facebook chat to pick up some African souvenirs (maybe head scarves) as gifts for my friends who had been taking such stellar care of me in his absence. Then, I added that instead, it would be *très excitant* to ask Max to house- and pet-sit so that I could meet up with him and his colleague either in the Hague, Zanzibar or Mozambique for a week or two. This was my cheapo move, my trap-setting chess strategy.

I also demurely invited him to be among a group of us making donations to cancer research in Nat's name, wondering how much he'd choose to contribute. I wasn't clowning around, but testing and challenging him to a game of explanation. Our conversation was cut off mid-sentence as I was typing the word 'donat—'.

Christmas came and went and what did I hear from him? Nothing, that's what! There was no news from the man. Then, just before New Year's, he wrote to say that he was sailing from Mafia Island southbound along the Tanzanian coast. He would likely be offshore, or at least away from power and the internet for a week. Still, he did wish me a healthy new year in advance. How thoughtful!

I had a houseful of guests for Christmas dinner, despite feeling crappy. The chemo was slashing at my energy, and I know that my forehead was always slightly creased. Good laughter without barbs in it became my costume, although my father, brother and his partner raised my sad meter—not for GJ, who they thought was saving Zanzibar, but for Nathalie. I was still very raw and being with my closest relatives brought all the sorrow back from that past Christmas with Nat. Max buffered the conversations as well as possible and helped with the meal and Dona pitched in to defer our thoughts from that tragedy, but I was exhausted and wanted only to sleep for the week. The others had no clue that I was not only mourning but also coping with

Walking on Heads

confusion, bewilderment and isolation from the burden of covering up for GJ and I was angry that he was treating me like a piece of poo on his shoe. The others were simply puzzled by GJ's prolonged work trip.

A part of me was feeling like a patsy for the first time in my life, letting someone walk all over me like the nice girl who finishes last. Little did GJ know, however, I would become Hurricane Patsy . . .

January contained more delays and excuses that in their way made sense, given that the man swore he was halfway around the world developing a supportive project to increase the capacity of Tanzanians to be more self-sufficient. What didn't make sense was his lack of connection to what was supposed to be our life. In reality, I was starting to see a new aspect to GJ: not the charming, appealing guy I first met, but an unhinged, unattractive nomad who had no scruples or consideration for others' feelings or assets.

The month whizzed by with more of the same. I was feeling dog-tired, partly from the chemical therapy for my disease and partially from dealing with a toddler dog. Dona was draining my energy and, although Maxine often walked her, I still had to be somewhat awake the rest of the day and rarely got to nap. And I was trying to put GJ out of my mind.

However, the Dutchman had been away since the fall, and my energy was up and down because the chemo was getting toxic. I was nauseous, and my fingers and toes were a tad numb as a cute little side effect. And my back often ached. Nevertheless, I could still type and so I sent GJ another note, wondering how he would deal with this one.

> Hey Dutchcosmo,
>
> I thought that I'd give you a little update about the coastal life of your Canadian.
>
> In no particular order, our Vancouver Canucks hockey heroes are 'Number 1' in the NHL and potentially far ahead of the pack statistically because of a number of

games in hand! How about that? Second news flash: we had a rat in the walls for a few days, scratching like crazy at night, until I called the pest management guys who found droppings in the attic but fortunately no damage. Traps were set and the entry hole was covered a day later so that the critter could make a getaway, and he/she did.

The third piece of my news involves Dona: I finally woke up and have found a dog trainer. Dona misses how you read the paper to her and longs for her walks with you. Luckily, your stand-in lives nearby and will make his first house call on Saturday. I am so excited to have our baby jump on the expert and try to take Joe for a walk. Nyahaha. I just can't handle Dona's strength and lack of obedience when walking anymore, which doesn't mean that she not a sweet good natured girl—just a tad deaf when she feels like it. The fourth thing is physiology: I have itchy palms and restless legs and incredibly soft lips ... today.

A

About a week later, sitting in my inbox was this piece that was supposed to make me feel better:

> Just one more task here for me in Africa. I am off to the interior to visit a few 'Millennium Villages' (UN project initiated by Jeffrey Sachs) as they have a comparable community development model. I basically disagree with their intentions but the ministry thought it wise to take a look.
>
> Oh boy, that wonderful dog of ours needs a man! You may be surprised but I am tired being here. Landscape

Walking on Heads

is stunning and work is inspiring, but some cool cold Georgia Straight breeze is what I long for, and some soft lips! :-) I won't be on the internet or phone until my return on Tuesday as there is hardly any electricity over there. Now want to leave Africa: it is getting harder and harder. :-(

Big kiss from Africa,
GJ

    I was so glad to have the diversion of my daughter to keep me from falling apart for the second time in the same year. I made a concerted effort to be totally available to Maxine without ever mentioning my fusion of emotions. She and Liana had separated, partly because Liana didn't understand why Max wasn't over her grieving, partly because of the girl/girl emotional and hormonal challenges and partly because relationships just aren't always a bed of roses.

    On top of that, her favourite uncle—Paul's brother, Tom—was very ill with a heart condition and Max was troubled about that. Max dealt with some of her feelings by making music, and it was during that time that she wrote a song for her sister called "Echo", which has been registered with SOCAN (a Canadian society of composers, authors and music publishers). This beautiful tune may hit the airwaves one day.

    My anxieties would have run Maxine into depression, including intense anger with GJ, so I zipped it and didn't mention him. If she fell apart any more, it would no doubt have pushed me over the edge, but as it was, I had the time and determination to focus my mind on the rabbit hole that GJ seemed to have bolted into.

    Curiouser and curiouser, GJ was running out of apologies for his delays and he was no longer asking about Maxine and Liana, or Dona, or me. I was considering taking up knitting when a few days later, something inexplicable bruised his English as he dropped this baffling line to me:

A Woman Scorned is Like a Rodeo Clown

> Something eerie is happening to my Facebook. It is being censored. No idea who is behind this. The NL warning was obviously correct, though frankly I think it is not the Islamists or the Russians but the USA operatives. Grrr...

He sounded drunk. It's true! This was clipped right out of his e-mail—in fact, it was the entire inebriated message. So, even though I had been enormously patient, to the nth degree, I now had to find some real answers to make riffs out of his white noise. I wasn't getting much comfort from him—in fact, it was as if reason had been kidnapped and replaced by illogical complications. Yep, I was dizzy, and it wasn't from a chemo cocktail or booze.

Earth to Grrr, I was thinking. How could I ground GJ and bring him back to reality and get the truth out of him? Was he just stalling me for some reason? Bryn and Ev were getting sick of asking about him, Maxine wouldn't even mention his name anymore and I was avoiding my stepdaughters, who were regularly asking delicately about his travels and return date.

In my darkened office, as the wind and rain hit my French windows, I figured that it was time to go back to my laptop and social networking, where I decided to share my dilemma about Dona with the MIA GJ. My walls reflected shadows of the wind and rain, as if they were encouraging me to venture on.

My lung had been filling with fluid again and the new chemo was making me very tired and buzzy, so sweet Dona was a huge responsibility. Given that she had more spunk than me in my condition, I knew that I would have to find a new home for her if GJ was not able to return. Max and my friends were doing their best to pitch in, but living with an enthusiastic, frisky dog 24/7 was not what I signed up for.

So I sent off a quick note called "Cloud of Pressure" as the rain smacked the house.

Walking on Heads

Dear GJ,

I had to hire a dog trainer for several private lessons to help Dona and me learn to walk better. She has nearly knocked me off my feet a couple of times and you can imagine how she still enthusiastically drags me to other dogs at the park. Also, she continues to dig holes in the garden and I'm afraid that she will escape again. I am tired of being a single doggie Mom and I need to know how you feel about me finding a new owner for her.

~A

He seemed to be on social networking often, but was logging off suddenly and repeatedly when I logged on. It felt like he didn't want to chat with me in real-time, and I carried around my thoughts about his shiftiness like a boa constrictor circling my neck. I needed to play with his reaction to my question or I felt like I would go mad.

Re. Cloud of Pressure

Hi there! Yes, you are right, it seems I keep you waiting. That, I realize, is agonizing, but it is totally unintentional.
    I am in Dodoma now and it is around 8:30 p.m. We have been operating from this town (long, hot and bumpy rides!), which is the official capital of the country. Tomorrow morning we fly to the Lake Victoria area to finally end up in Dar again on Tuesday. It is all quite interesting, but the overall experience is forcing me to revisit my original ideas about how to create a community project here. While travelling and doing these field trips I also read a lot of theoretical stuff on development aid

A Woman Scorned is Like a Rodeo Clown

varying from reports to books. Still quite impressed by Schumacher's *Small is Beautiful*! but now also digesting and incorporating theories of a number of others.

All in all, this stay here is pretty overwhelming and indeed, I sort of lose sight of the home front. Frankly I am also under a cloud of pressure, though obviously a different one: the project characteristics attract a lot of attention of policy makers in Holland (I now even have to respond to questions of MPs and senators). The ministry thinks the project should make use of the present momentum and pushes me forward. This is nice of course, but it destabilizes my plans for my own (and thus: our) future. I am expected to report back in the Hague and Brussels on Thursday. After that, I want to fly back to Canada.

By the way: the ministry has urged us not to in any way reveal where we are, as long as we are in 'terrorist-active' countries like Tanzania, and particularly shy away from social networking sites like the Facebook wall. So I removed your wall post :-((I think the fear is somewhat overdone, but the reputation of the present NL government is indeed not very positive over here).

I am very happy you are doing well with respect to the treatment! But somehow I always felt you still have a very active life ahead of you! And, please darling, I don't want you to give up our beautiful Dona! She needs her strong man back as do you. I am off to a late dinner now; I hope I can have a not so spicy dish, as it is already hot enough here! Talk to you soon!

Big hugs and kisses,
GJ

Walking on Heads

I decided to not respond. It took a few days before I called my friend Bryn wondering if there was another reason he didn't want wall posts that all his friends could see, or chats with me. Was it because I might ask the question? Interesting enough, he had deleted an innocent post that Bryn had placed two weeks before which simply affirmed, "Your Vancouver friends miss you!"

She and her husband knew us well as a couple, and she was one of my sounding boards whenever I would try to explain GJ's delays that kept on and on and on. In spite of her busy schedule as a coach for entrepreneurial women, she said that she would message him and see if all was well—in other words, find out where the hell he was.

She heard back right away, which shocked us both, and I immediately received a sister message from him:

> We finally arrived in Arusha! Took long and was a tough drive. Had some adventures at the border and one annoying police control in Tanzania. We bluffed our way through. :-) And we had a flat tyre, too. In the middle of nowhere. Now off to bed. At least the hotel is fine and the bed comfortable. Pfff. We decide to sleep in as it is now almost daylight.
>
> GJ

Did I hear an echo? Here was another entry for my 'Hmmm' file. I thought that I had been serenaded by this story before—the border-bluffing fiasco/flat-tire hassle had already happened once in the Balkans, hadn't it? Never mind . . . I believe in cultivating a nourishing inner voice and finding some peace from the slings and arrows of outrageous crooning by welcoming a little meditation.

After a few slow sun salutations, my mind had permission to warm up again and I took in the benefit of breathing into a few seated twists and

A Woman Scorned is Like a Rodeo Clown

inverted poses. I just love navel-gazing while my neck is being massaged by gravity. My mind can float.

Anni, trust your gut and get to the bottom of this debris he is flinging around. You deserve more than his cavalier crap about delays, delays and more fucking delays. Clearly, yoga doesn't edit my words so much as my inner clarity.

Subsequently, I alighted from the floor and Googled his name, feeling thick for not having thought of it before. Then, I had never checked out anyone I actually knew, except an older colleague once who claimed to have gone to jail for supporting the 'Ban the Bomb' movement. Surfing is easy, but incredibly frustrating when someone who should be a someone does not show up. There was a Goos Jank who was an undertaker, and there were three accountants, two German scientists and a writer also sharing his name, but none who worked with the Netherlands government.

I became a modern sleuth. I wished that I had written down Jana's and Marie's last names from that old sneak into GJ's e-mail account, but I hadn't, so I tried our favourite social networking site and tapped in to GJ's old school friend Arne DeGroote, who had the same last name as a Latin teacher of mine from high school.

Arne and I had spoken once on the phone, when he called from his conference on town planning at the Pan Pacific Hotel. I had not met him during his visit to Vancouver though, because I had just started intravenous chemo and had been feeling lousy, but GJ had enjoyed a great lunch, care of his old pal Arne. Also, GJ had chronicled how Arne's twenty-year relationship with a man was very co-dependent, so Arne could not stay for an extra day or two, which was why he never came to visit us.

I had never checked anyone's e-mail before that year and there I was, heading for another first. I went rogue and sent a plucky note introducing myself and my situation, enquiring if Arne knew if GJ was okay. Just asking . . .

Walking on Heads

Hi Arne,

We both know Goos, and I feel like I know you a bit through him. I am sorry that I didn't get to meet you when you came to Vancouver for your conference.

I am sending this because I am puzzled as to whether Goos ever made it to Africa after his keynote speech in the Hague in October. He has sent many notes to me about some work he is caught up in and about his plans to return to Vancouver soon.

But, lack of money to pay his part while staying with me because he had lost his wallet has put me in a tough spot wondering . . . has he really been working halfway across the world or not? I miss his company as well as the money he owes me. Please advise. By the way, I am not crazy, but feel anxious and worried about him because I continuously get different stories. Thanks for your patience with my situation.

Warm regards,
Anni

8
Sixteen! Sixteen!

We may have all come on different ships, but we're in the same boat now.
—Martin Luther King Jr.—

Sixteen is the natural number following fifteen, a composite number and a square number. It is the age of consent in some countries, and often the age where one can legally learn to drive a car. For those living on the British Columbia coast, "Sixteen!" is the announcement made on ferries suggesting that passengers prepare to disembark. It was, coincidentally, the date when I got the lowdown on GJ online.

One piece that still puzzles me was his wall-posting on Facebook as his Valentine's gesture, one day after V-day. It was a picture of a young Anne with their Lippizaner horse. "If I ever loved an animal, it would be this beauty standing with my wife." I swear he was not on chemo, but he was drivelling like he was—either that, or drinking heavily. This caused my eyes to smart and dilate, and I rarely drink. Oh, sweet Lord, please send me a sign. Another . . . better sign.

Hallelujah! On February 16th, I received the long-awaited message . . . but it was from GJ's friend, with not quite the content I was prepared for. I was glad that I was already sitting down and that I had a warm cup of tea at the ready.

Walking on Heads

I took to aggravating my cuticles and chewing my top lip as I read:

> I am as puzzled as you are. I am not aware of Goos's travel to Holland or Africa and doubt whether he has been there recently. In fact, I thought he was in Toronto with Marie. At least, that is what he told me. Although I love him dearly, I am afraid he sometimes has difficulties distinguishing reality from fiction. He is a great story teller. Anything he says about his personal life and work I take with a grain of salt. But that is easier for me than it must be for you being his partner (are you?). I am a bit worried about the financial part. Never having bothered recovering his lost credit cards could mean that he didn't have any, which could mean that there are financial problems. Could this perhaps have been a reason for him to leave Vancouver? Unable to cope with the reality that was about to catch up with him? I do not know, Anni, but I do realize that my reply is perhaps not very helpful or reassuring. Don't hesitate to call me if you want: +31-***-******.
>
> Best regards,
> Arne

Truth be told (I can't bear that phrase now), GJ had been in Toronto since he left me! The confusing part was that the same morning that Arne finally responded to my note, GJ e-mailed to say that he was returning from Africa in two weeks. And I learned later that he had also sent Maxine a note suggesting a musician that she would like, saying that he would return soon. That moment was the first where I felt mindfully familiar with feeling dim-witted and semi-conscious. I felt sick in my guts and sad in my heart that I had spent so much time worrying about this phantom man

Sixteen! Sixteen!

instead of mourning for Nathalie. And he had lied to my Maxine about where he was! He had lied about intending to ever return my money! Was Arne really gay with a needy partner? Were my kaleidoscope eyes a lie? Who was he and did he ever work?

There were simply too many puzzle pieces and questions buzzing around my head. How would he explain himself? Should I ever get the chance to have him in front of me? It was then that I remembered the duffle luggage bags that he'd dragged into the airport as he threw me kisses. Those mammoth bags had had little nametags marked 'Marie something-or-other'. Had that box of electronics in my garage with a stranger's handwriting marking it 'GJ'S STUFF' been courtesy of Marie packing his junk while kicking him out? Or had she been sending him to me so that I could take care of him for a while?

So, imp that I can be, straight away I e-mailed GJ saying I had been informed that he was in Toronto and I wondered if I might foist Dona off on him and Marie! By the way, the verb 'foist' comes from a phrase in a Dutch dialect: *vuisten*, meaning 'fist', as in concealing dice in one's hand during crapshoot.

As I was shaking out my clenched fists and staring at my cuticles, it seemed like only minutes before this note arrived from nametag-Marie, obviously reacting to GJ's news that I was upset:

> We have not talked but this has been all quite awkward, really. GJ and I have had much more than an intellectual relationship together and he was not being completely honest with either of us last year. He told me that you knew that he had returned to me in the fall. As a woman who deeply empathized with your situation, I eventually accepted that the cosmos had mysterious ways and lessons for us all . . . and I believe that we are all the better for his decision to have been there with you—and for you.

Walking on Heads

I intuited it was a deep and meaningful experience for him to be there in your community of friends and family and to be by your side as a friend. I do not know what to say to you except that, after thinking about it very carefully, we are planning to stay together. But I believe that I, too, can be an ally and resource for you—at least I think so. I hope you are feeling better and that things are going well for you. You are a very courageous and strong woman and have faced so much. I hope that this year is lighter for you. Please feel free to contact me if there is any way I can be of help.

Warm wishes,
Marie

He phoned me within ten minutes of the e-mail from Marie. My guess is that she told him to! Like a self-conscious little boy, all he did was mutter, with a tone of voice I had never heard before. "Allo? . . . I'm sorry . . . I fucked up . . . "

Like a cheeky little girl, I took my time, counted to ten and reacted with, "Yes, you . . . certainly did. How long have you been in Toronto?"

"I've just been here three weeks . . . "

"And you were going to tell me about that . . . when?" I sped up. "I would like you to come here and tell me to my face why you led me on."

He countered with, "I would have to bring Marie with me . . . "

My tongue was as quick as one of his famous left-handed tennis serves. "You know, you are the second rat that has infested my world this year! I hope you and Marie both have hantaviruses! . . . Goodbye."

And I hung up. It was a pleasure to feel him twitch through the phone line. Then, I irrationally wondered how Marie had felt about the nostalgic yearning for his good times with Caroline he'd planted on his Facebook wall in November, or how she had handled the strange Lippizan Valentine post.

Sixteen! Sixteen!

What a heartless guttersnipe, to say that he had scarcely unpacked in Toronto when Marie had just written that he had been camping out with her since the fall! As Henry Higgins said to Eliza, "I have my own spark of divine fire," so I gathered myself with a few slow breaths and shed the bedraggled slurs that were lining up in my mind.

I shared Marie's e-mail with Ev, who called to emphasize that GJ's roommate sounded like she'd been doused with something, maybe synthetic medicinal therapy. Just as we were marvelling in stupefaction over her, I received another note from the mysterious Marie.

> One other thing—I had requested (repeatedly) that he inform you of his actions and that he take responsibility for his decisions by being truthful. He told me he had done this and that you understood that he probably would not be back. Although he insisted it was a delicate and messy situation and he has been trying to take care of your feelings, I assured him the best way to take care of someone was to be honest. (For all his charm, he is very unsure of himself.) Your e-mail indicated that this was not done. I am sorry—for both of us—but I really need rest from all this!
>
> M

"After thinking about it very carefully?"
... "Probably would not be back?"
... "Unsure of himself?"
... "Messy?"

It seemed obvious to Ev and me that he hadn't made up his mind during the winter and that Marie had no idea that he had been deceiving me about his 'travels' and intention to return. If she really believed that he had done me a favour as a friend, though, by sharing a meaningful experience, what was messy? I felt very sorry for her, as his second choice (and maybe not for the first time). GJ was probably actually being honest when he said that she was in love with him but he didn't feel the same. She also appeared to be the mother-figure in their relationship, concerned about his insecurity and telling him what to do. A part of me hoped that he in fact cared for her and that he would stay with this keen woman and maybe quit with the lies. So what if he thought that he was a huge planet and women were moons orbiting around him? I know that I did not want to see or touch that guy again, not even with a ten-foot pole.

Did he actually possibly think that he had done me a favour by helping out and that he owed me nothing, not even an explanation? If he had been a woman, would I have felt so violated? These questions percolated in a healthy mind that couldn't possibly imagine using someone else's kindness by lying about one's intentions. A pathological liar who planned and used another person could be male or female. I mulled over whether a guy would allow a woman to walk all over him and I realized: yes and no. It would depend on the circumstances and the lies. The kicker is that being chronically irresponsible is different from living a life that is an out-and-out falsehood, and neither sex would sanction that behaviour being palmed off on them once they figured out the liar's way of life.

Should I have encouraged GJ to explain to me (by himself, without Marie's hand in his) why he had teased me so many times, especially about his extended trip and about his desire to return? This was a ridiculous inner exercise, because there was no molecule of doubt in my mind that any written or verbal explanation from him would contain nothing except more and more deceit, because he could not legitimize his decisions to lead me on without exposing himself.

Back in my university days, before I got practical and did graduate work in teaching, I once had a longing to be a writer. Unfortunately, the launch of my book, *Motherwords*, had been put on hold because of Nathalie's death and my immobilization from mourning her. So after lashing back at GJ with the juvenile hantavirus remark (while wiping

Sixteen! Sixteen!

my nose, gritting my teeth and gnawing on the "doused" comment and Marie's naïve e-mails to me), he got the brunt of some of my pent-up writer's angst.

All these reflections triggered an obligation to open the Christmas bottle of chocolate port, for its non-synthetic caffeine rush and its decadent taste and to loosen my clenched jaw. I wrote a short story about a man in harmony with his fiction and out of sync with his pyramid of lies. It flowed out of me like the Tigris and Euphrates were overflowing their dams to become one vast body of water.

I created "The Undignified Tale of the Lost Wallet" in the style of a fairytale. Then, before I got cold feet, I immediately messaged it to GJ and to Marie (who was in the dark about GJ's *in flagrante delicto* e-mails and debts to me), then I CC'd it to all my close girlfriends as witnesses so GJ and Marie would know that the group of us knew about his immoral behaviour, including his financial obligations. I knew that I would never see a dime from him, but it seemed that maybe, just maybe, Marie would at least think twice about sheltering and coddling a crook and a liar. The point of sending the e-mail was to make it very clear that this episode with GJ would have no chance for a repeat engagement. It was my proclamation: I was no longer waiting for Godot or keeping his secrets and lies to myself.

9

Never Let the Same Dog Bite You Twice

In the book of life, the answers aren't in the back.
— Charles Schultz —

After we split, my ex-husband Paul would sometimes say that there is no happiness in love except at the end of an English novel.

GJ immediately blocked me and my friends on Facebook. I thought that it was his way of removing us from his past. Instead, I now know that he did it as insurance against any of us posting something incriminating on his wall for the world—including his next conquests—to see. Ironically, we had not thought of posting something caustic, but later we wished we had. Add another irony, which is that those pretty little privacy settings on social networking sites protect cheaters from being noticed as much as they protect us moral people from spammers.

Following huge blubbers of confusion, embarrassment and foolishness with my girlfriends about the way I had been duped and used as a fallback for GJ's plans, I finally started to breathe again. I have never doubted that he would have tried to return to me once Marie tired of him. I was aghast that this man who had seemed so supportive and sincere could have lied and used me, particularly when I was in deep mourning and battling—as the overused saying goes—my own health crisis.

Walking on Heads

I was suffering the twin reactions of shock and dismay that there was to be no happy ending to this story ... about my bank account, which was in a sorry state. So I bit the bullet and asked for a line of credit from my bank. This almost triggered energetic constipation. I knew that I was practically at a standstill and that I had to do something else to get my entrails to shift.

My first inclination was to recycle everything that GJ had left behind ... after checking whether there might be anything valuable to sell or barter. I set forth to purge the house of him. It was not a crusade, in that I didn't need to remove everything from the surroundings that reminded me of him instantly. In fact, I was quite calm and focused on reclaiming my space and my life and my dignity. It was, ironically, somehow refreshing.

There wasn't much, but by the weekend I had dumped out the paltry contents of his drawers, chucking them into my recycling bag and thinking, "Is this all there is to the end of a hot relationship ... a few mismatched socks, a couple of T-shirts, a European hair dryer, a stained pair of briefs, old worn shoes, tennis gear and a box of junk in the garage?"

As I moved on with the elimination of him from my environment with the calm of a Buddhist nun (as opposed to King Ghidorah, the three-headed monster), I slowly and deliberately made two piles of his clothes: one was for Bryn's tall husband, the other for the thrift shop. There was an ease to using the redistribution of his worldly goods as a way of dispersing the ions that made up the mystery man. Then I emptied out the faux-leather briefcase that he had left in my office. He had made such a big deal of taking the *'Nederlands Olympisch Comité * Nederlandse Sport Federatie'* case with him, like a boy proud of his new watch. Consequently, he had left the old case, along with its miserable contents.

As I blasted Queen through the house, I started tidying the case, relieving it of two pens, an old napkin from the Water's Edge Bar & Grill and a couple of empty mickeys of vodka. Next, as I sang "We are the Champions", I checked out the inner zippered pocket. I was relieved that there was nothing dead or mummified inside, such as one of last year's wolf spiders. In fact, it was empty.

Never Let the Same Dog Bite You Twice

I promise that I have not made this next part up. I had almost tossed all the offal from the bag into the wastebasket when my curiosity—or rather, my intuition—triggered a magical bit of sleight of hand. In the outer zippered pocket on the case, I found two pieces of folded paper that would change the course of the next phase of my life. Lightly resting in my hot little hands was the key piece to unravelling the inscrutable GJ.

As a teacher, I was used to poring over homework papers, so I opened the pages expecting doodles or notes for his project or phone numbers or even an abandoned love note. What I found was a phantom receipt for who-knows-what, as well as proof of payment for a European cellphone with a 'telemoveis Vodafone' header. Both chits were in a language that I didn't recognize right away, but I did recognize the racing heartbeat of elation.

The cellphone invoice was not made out to GJ, but to the woman I had heard him speak of as Jana. Her full name (Janapada Arrais), her address and even her birthdate were listed, and I knew—I just knew—that I had a lead. I did the Snoopy happy dance in my head, even though the paper felt suddenly like concrete.

The feelings in my body that evening after finding the clue to GJ's past were like those when one has just come to after fainting. I was light-headed, my heart was picking up pace and almost getting ahead of my breathing and I felt nauseous. Yet I also felt the adrenaline rush of an investigative journalist onto a good story.

"GJ, GJ, GJ . . . how could you donate this clue? I thought you were a smart man and that you knew what you were doing when you ran off like the cowardly lion." I presumed to also answer for him, he with the cold steel-blue eyes: "Anni, Anni, Anni . . . get over it. Being ditched and feeling scorned is messy, but you'll find someone else."

Disbelief and disappointment just about covers how I felt when I understood that he had left in a spineless, deceitful way, but what I found gave body rushes a whole new definition.

After the discovery of the receipts, I took my cellphone into my bathtub, full of me and a jigger of bubble bath. I needed to call somebody.

Walking on Heads

My number one priority in renovating the house had been to add my own private soaker tub, which had soothed more than sore muscles on several other heart-wrenching occasions. It caught many, many of my tears after Nathalie died.

As I lounged in the hot, fragrant water, I closed my eyes and then dialled Evangeline, begging her for an alien starship to take me away from this harrowing world. Of course I insisted that she make sure I was clothed, but at that point I was still shivering from my bodily reactions to the reply from GJ's friend Arne. Mostly, all I muttered to Ev was, "Help!"

I was feeling betrayed, embarrassed, angry, lonely and pruney. I had stayed in the water too long and I needed a map or plan or . . . something. So I towelled off, and was heading back to my home office and the internet when Ev rang the bell and entered the house like a dervish on a mission. She was juggling a bottle of icewine and a bag of cheeses and various crackers along with her signature giant bag. She was in for the long haul.

We hugged, snivelled, poured glasses of wine and laughed ourselves cross-eyed. What kind of a turd lives off other women, we guffawed? Who gets away with big fat fabricated stories about their careers and extraordinary accomplishments? He who ranted about shysters who (as the Dutch would say) show off with others' feathers? What did he buy with the cash I gave him? A Hudson's Bay parka . . . dental work . . . several new pairs of tennis shoes? What kind of insect would sink its teeth into a family in deep mourning? That was when I choked a little on a dry seeded cracker and Ev raced to get me a glass of water.

For a few hours we laughed, yelled and devised ways of embarrassing him until we fell asleep on the couch. Evangeline was gone when I awoke. I sauntered into the kitchen for cereal, coffee, headache pills and leftover tuna for the animals. Dona had been remarkably empathetic and hadn't disturbed my rest, although she had also been up late the night before with us.

Then, despite the gorgeous green day, I grabbed a cushy pillow for my back and planted myself in front of my laptop. I didn't want to take the computer to bed with me in case my forays in search of more information

Never Let the Same Dog Bite You Twice

stained the sanctuary of my bedding and set my sleep patterns awry. I sat at the desk where GJ had cheated and I prepared to find some answers. It is so interesting that there are only a few ages—maybe those under five and those over eighty-five—who do not rely on computers as a function of their lives. I have been amazed by the number of young elementary students who have cellphones and their own computers. They can't even bring them to class until secondary school, but what I'm saying is that our lives now revolve around a much more complex set of connections than when I was a young student.

It made perfect sense to go back to social networking and search for the Portuguese woman, Janapada Arrais. First of all, there was no poet with her name, but there were eight women sharing it. I nominated three who looked about our age and, at seven in the evening, Pacific Standard Time, I sent a gentle message:

> Do you know Goos Jank? My name is Anni Mills and I live in Canada. I am wondering if you might be the Jana who lived with GJ in Braga in 2008? If so, it would be good to chat about him with you. Otherwise, I apologize for disturbing you.
>
> Warm regards,
> Anni

The next morning—and I mean early morning: 5:00 a.m. my time when I woke up and checked!—there was a message from one of the Janas:

> Yes, click on friendship and you can tell me what time we should be online.
>
> Kind regards,
> J

Walking on Heads

Immediately, I typed a note back to this foreign woman:

> Thank you for your quick reply, Jana. I hope that this isn't too hard for you. We might chat in the evening. My noon hour is about 9 p.m. for you and I can be home at that time.

Within twenty minutes, I had a response:

> I appreciate your kindness although there is no reason to be so troubled about me. If you give me your phone number, I will call you directly.
>
> Hear you soon,
> J

10
Travel Changes Nothing Except the Location

The true hypocrite is the one who ceases to perceive his deception, the one who lies with sincerity.
— André Gide —

I was just thinking of letting the cat and dog out when the phone rang. The chirrup of the telephone didn't sound any different than usual, but for some reason it startled me when the call display registered "UNKNOWN". I, who usually ignore the unknowns because of telemarketers, picked up and took a breath and a long on-purpose pause before saying, "Hello?"

There was an equally pregnant pause on the other end before I heard a melodious voice say, "Anni? . . . This is Jana."

Jana had been as hesitant as I was, but in her case, it was because she was enormously fearful and anxious that I was him! She needed to hear my voice before accepting that it was safe to continue to talk. I was stunned that she was fearful that he was stalking her.

Southern European people have a reputation for being very enthusiastic and emotional, especially compared to quiet unassertive Canadians, and Jana was just that. Once she knew I was me, she speed-talked for almost an hour without me saying much except, "Oh . . . I'm so sorry . . . that's terrible," and then "Oh" again many more times.

Walking on Heads

The he who had been my gorgeous, charming boyfriend had also been her boyfriend and was . . . a disturbed, twisted man. My skin went cold and rippled as I listened. I just couldn't believe that he was a mental case. I thought that maybe she was the deranged one, until I remembered that I had contacted her! At the edge of her voice was not craziness, but emotional turbulence, as she was dragged back into her stories of GJ.

Jana didn't essentially explain anything in any order and kept jumping from topic to topic, sometimes repeating herself for effect. I knew that she was smart, that it was the trauma dervish that had shocked and taken over her tongue. So I tried to hang on and make some sense of the jumbled pieces of her nonstop monologue.

This is kind of how the soliloquy panned out:

At the beginning of their union, GJ was a kind, charming man who had been introduced by her cousin, who told her that GJ was a great guy. The men met while walking the Way of St. James in Spain. (This part I already knew.) Jana said that GJ was kind and considerate with her children and charismatic amongst her community of artistic friends. He had pretended—and she stressed that word—to have credentials from the Society for International Development's Netherlands Branch, exploring the migration problems of people from the third world to more developed societies. He boasted that his work had sent him to various countries.

It had been his healthy body, his gifted mind and the fact that her male cousin had vetted him that made it easy to fall for him.

Even though Jana was talking faster than my brain could compute, I did pick up that the two had travelled together at her expense and that they had attended many art shows and plays. The Jerk, as she called him, had cheated on her with a well-known painter from Golegã, and in fact—although she hadn't known it at the time—he had also been cheating on his long-time Dutch girlfriend, Barbra, with her.

His lies to her were many. One was that he was an expert on the Balkans and international development. Another was that he had been married for fifteen years and had five children by the woman named

Travel Changes Nothing Except the Location

Barbra. Yet another was that his Eurobank card had been stolen, which left him cashless for months.

He additionally claimed that most of his possessions, including valuable art, were in a storage unit in Utrecht, and that he would deal with her money troubles. Her money troubles? She fumed that she was a respected businesswoman who taught part-time at the university in Coimbra.

I also learned through her ranting that once, when she was pushy (my word, not hers) with GJ about his lack of euros and possessions, he had shoved her very forcefully against a door frame in a flare of annoyance.

My bum was getting numb and my neck was stiffening, so I walked around the house while Jana carried on. I learned that she had indeed been chasing GJ for a couple of years. She was on his case, but it was for the money he owed her!

Despite having a Ph.D in Social Sciences and not being the airy-fairy poet that he had hinted at, she had supported him and allowed him to borrow money to buy a couple of paintings, which he had sent away to be appraised by an art dealer in Germany. That was the money she wanted from him, because she was quite sure that he had sold the two pieces. The short story was that he had pocketed the profits and hung his head like a sad puppy when she demanded the truth . . . and then slapped him. Twice.

He threatened to go to the authorities (with a claim that Jana should lose custody of her kids for being a delinquent mother) if she didn't stop with the harassing questions. That was when Jana smacked him again (giving him a significant nosebleed), threw his meagre things out the window and had her brother and cousin escort him out of the city. I thought to myself, *I wish that I had done that!*

That exchange was just an opener. There was a plethora of upsetting details, regarding more women not unlike me, into which I would be plummeted.

Marie, strangely enough, was scattered throughout Jana's tirade. A most disconcerting piece of the puzzle, in fact, was this other Canadian woman of his. She sat in the midst of the GJ drama like an umbra. She has been a phantom for me, not physically present but an eccentric player and a recurring image that goaded me and apparently aggravated Jana as well.

It turns out that Canadian Marie had been GJ's part-time lover back in the Balkans before he met Jana in Portugal. Marie had been working there when GJ took a detour from a visit to Holland and met Jana's cousin on the Way of St. James. As soon as he met Jana, he fell for the gorgeous, impetuous younger Portuguese lady, who conveniently happened to have a second home near Sarajevo which she had inherited from her mother. He insinuated himself into her life, miscalculating her fierce determination to protect her children and herself. Then, after Jana tossed him out, GJ had scooted back to Marie, who was wrapping up her work so they had both aimed their lives towards Canada.

And, no surprise here: GJ was not Marie's Ph.D advisor. Marie had to know that, although GJ had been unofficially involved in her Canadian work as a volunteer, he did not work for a living or have a steady income (although Jana suspected that he may have still had some of the money that he had inherited from his father).

Here's one of the most confusing elements for me. Marie knew about Jana's incidents with GJ, because Jana had e-mailed and called her in Canada a couple of times regarding GJ's debts and his ongoing pestering messages after she had kicked him out. Jana warned Marie to take care. Marie had been tipped off about his mouldy actions by Jana and, as it turned out, by another ex, who had the guts to send her information on the traits of antisocial personalities. Marie had not reacted, except to say that the two lovers were not in hiding and to stridently notify the women that she couldn't handle their points of view and not to bother her with their problems.

Even though I realize that Jana's messages probably seem a bit hysterical, there were reasons. Jana sent Marie one more message, reminding her of GJ's trail of debris. Perhaps because it was so unbelievably disturbing, or because Marie wanted to save GJ from himself, or because she was in denial or jealous of the beautiful women, Marie seemed to

Travel Changes Nothing Except the Location

have had her sleeping mask on her mind or over her heart. We could only speculate as to why she didn't look the shyster in the face.

Jana felt strongly that Marie was either a lovesick enabler or possessed of a mothering complex, which shed light on why she accepted him back time and again. I didn't even want to venture into that pathology. All I knew was that most of the things he had told me—and indeed, much of our relationship—were built on misrepresentations and illusions. Marie's experience with him couldn't be too much different.

Marie knew that GJ had spent a couple of months with me when they first arrived in Canada, long before my health crisis, because I had asked for him several times when she had answered the phone. And she knew that GJ had run to me after he left her just after the Olympics, because I overheard a couple of their heated conversations. She knew that I was more than a friend, but GJ must have convinced her otherwise. Most likely, GJ had persuaded her of his distorted version that the lost wallet story was a figment of my imagination and that he had stayed at my request. How interesting that this technique is called 'gaslighting', and that GJ was fascinated yet appalled when politicians and corporations used that same tactic. Gaslighting is a form of psychological abuse in which false information is presented to victims with the intent of making them doubt their own memories and perceptions, and I'm in no doubt that it was in his own bag of handy, often-used tricks!

Jana was livid that Marie had not warned me about him and his past escapades, because she had heard about or witnessed many of them. I didn't need that kind of friendship when I was already dealing with my grief and my health challenges! We agreed that I would have put two and two together and rejected his flimsy income and his lack of integrity and moral fibre, had I known. I would have launched him back at Marie, or into Lost Lagoon with all its goose poop.

The howl of the wolf in sheep's clothing was getting louder, almost thunderous. The conversation with Jana had stretched on for what seemed like a decade. I would rather have been gardening or even cleaning my oven, but I hung in there (with my "American" speech pattern, as she called it) and kept shaking my head and prompting her for more details about GJ as I paced around the house.

In the midst of her monologue, she alerted me that I should change all my passwords, because GJ had hounded and hacked into Barbra's private e-mails and documents and was still trying to keep an eye on them both. So I headed to my office as I listened, wondering how would Jana know Barbra so well, who one might think should be her rival.

"You know Barbra?" I had to ask upfront.

I can only explain the impact as being surreal as I learned that Jana knew both Barbra, who is a photographer (not an hotelier) in Amsterdam, and Annelies, who is a dietician in Rotterdam (not a doctor in Belgium)! They had, in fact, been connected to each other by GJ's sons, who were now keeping their distance from their father's antics.

Jana was talking five hundred words a minute and her volume escalated as I rapidly learned that GJ's twin sons would have little to do with him, partly because he had filched their trust funds when they were in their teens and partly because they knew from their aunt that GJ had mortgaged their grandfather's property and spent the money that had been eventually meant for both him and their aunt. His sons were made aware by their mother that GJ was messed up—not necessarily dangerous, just disturbed. In fact, they hardly ever heard directly from their father.

The sun outside my window was setting while my brain was rising up in protest against his attachment issues. The break in my inner storm cloud came with the welcome newsflash that GJ's sons were remarkable—in a good way. They were well-adjusted, fine young men. Daniel was working towards a graduate degree in sports physiology while the other, Michiel, planned to write his dissertation in psychology on ASPD (the 'Hitler syndrome'). Apparently, studying the pathology is a classic recovery tactic for the children of troubled personalities.

When I listened to Jana, I knew that she was clearly telling me about my Dutchman, since I had already heard the other women's names and

Travel Changes Nothing Except the Location

some details about his sons from GJ's own mouth. I just hadn't heard that he was a liar. I didn't know that his twin boys were afraid for him, because someday someone might take retribution on him for his transgressions.

The young men knew both Annelies and Barbra (who was not their mother, as Jana had been led to believe). The boys had sporadically visited with their father at each of the women's homes when they were younger. They had been well-adjusted, playful guys, arriving with neatly folded, clean clothes, obviously well-cared for by their mother Anne. Both of the former girlfriends had kept in touch with the young men and still loved and cared about them.

It was through GJ's sons that Annelies had eventually contacted Barbra, and also through them that the two exes had paid Jana a visit after he had left her. They had thought about telling Jana about his behaviour while GJ was living with her in Braga, but knew that they were being portrayed by him as neurotic. And as I thought, Barbra had still been bristling after being unkindly discarded for Jana.

So Jana, Barbra and Annelies eventually formed a friendship triad because of their common abuser. That is not to say that GJ was or is a hard-nosed psychopath, but he most definitely is a man who is out of touch with his true self, as he decadently goes forth and twists lives with 'Drosted' deceptions and illusions.

The European ladies' encounters were not dissimilar from mine, but Jana had also had the revolting experience of being injured in front of her children and had suffered the anxiety of facing GJ's escalated frustrations. Barbra, on the other hand, had sensed his inner mayhem and had been too afraid to make any wrong moves when he was with her; she had played dead, in a sense. After hearing about me through Jana, Barbra sent me this message:

> Act rationally, not emotionally. Try to get Marie on your side. Send her FB request. Block HIM on FB, you can always unblock later. He cannot accept that his victim

is discovering the truth about him. He will try to find out your plans, he will tell that you are jealous about Marie and you are crazy (he might say cancer therapy changed your brain, he helped you so much!!) He will repeat the Jana/Barbra scenario, two women fighting with each other—Be careful and break completely any contact with him. NO TALKS/NO MEETINGS. He is not a real criminal but an experienced liar and there is no punishment against his deeds. Freak told me that Jana was ill and he felt responsible for her. That is why he needed to meet her and take care of her. I was presented to Jana as a mentally disturbed and a very, very jealous mother of his several children. This narcissistic waste presents himself as a man of duty and responsibility.

Unbelievably, Jana also was still—yes, still—dealing with a constant stream of e-mails from him. That was when I sat and listened extremely carefully. She told me that he was messaging her weekly, supposedly from Tanzania, asking for her to let him come back to her—a manoeuvre he had also used with Barbra five years before. She said that she would forward some of those e-mails to me and to Marie, about whom she blurted with frustration, "That stupideh, stupideh woman!" I already knew he was in contact with Jana from that innocent snitch into GJ's e-mails months ago. She spat that he was likely, at this point, looking for his next free ride to Easy Street.

II
All Together Now

Knowing is not enough; we must apply.
Willing is not enough; we must do.
—Johann Wolfgang von Goethe—

From our weird launch into a friendship, Jana included both Barbra and Annelies in our gyrating liaisons through e-mail messages. Then, when convenient, we all moved on to using Skype, but mostly we continued with our barrage of e-mails and Facebook messages. We had a heyday comparing notes and insulting his character. They each spoke and wrote decent English which I was very grateful for, although sometimes we got our wires crossed. The rash of minutiae I received from the women made my brain swirl like it was being worked on with a hand blender. When the diatribe ended, it verified that he was permanently broken inside and that he was the pitiable one, not us.

The next evening after a number of interchanges, when I thanked them for their willingness to revisit their own traumas, we all licked our wounds together and bid each other decent dreams. The next day, Barbra had obviously been stewing over her fears, because she sent us a short yet urgent message that shook my insides:

> I will make another e-mail account and will let you know the new address. With my Hotmail when I log in there is a new e-mail it shows as 'read'! is GJerk our little sociopath behind it??

This was the first that I heard him stamped with that harsh medical term and it took weeks more to really believe that the man with choirboy looks and gentle laughter was a walking trespasser.

I needed a storyboard to keep all the facts straight. While recording my new allies' statements in teacher's shorthand, I tried to find something to guffaw over, which was my way of dealing with my nerves. We had agreed that we had the same opinions on his sloppiness, his drinking, his obsession with his hair and goatee, and that his good looks were fading. Still, only a few small things at this point genuinely amused us. In fact, many of the details had scarred our consciousnesses, as if the Joker had been going at us with his bladed playing cards.

I nattered into my mirror for a week, trying to make sense of what I knew was just the tip of the iceberg of cold elements these women had to share. We had become four women on two separate continents in three countries who had been friends with benefits with the handsome, charming GJ. Now, we were CC'ing each other like dazzling comic-book heroines.

Since I felt like I was getting cauliflower ear from all the telephoning, I involved my BFFs to cut down on the number of times I had to tell all the details over and over. These dear ladies had already witnessed my waiting game over the winter and they had each read my undignified tale about the missing wallet, so inviting my close girlfriends in on the exchanges made total sense and expanded the new sisterhood to ten: the four of us survivors plus my cousin Ev and my friends Bryn, Liz, Linsey, Nicole and Marcia.

My network here in British Columbia had a list of things in common with our new European girlfriends: we were all willing to be honest and supportive with each other and to laugh our asses off when we needed

All Together Now

to, or yank one another back from the pity abyss. They may have been as besieged with the facts as I was, but my girlfriends were sturdy and unwilling to let me go through this horror show alone and very sensitive to how drained my body and mind were from sweeping up all the details.

The most heartbreaking fine point that set us 'chosen ones' apart from my girlfriends, however, was that we had been available and exposed when the sociopath GJ had picked us off. Our vulnerability had been taken into temporary custody by his neediness and, although it could have happened to any of us in that situation, it had happened to us four. Cracks in our lives had been the ready set-up for him and he had gentled himself into each of our cushy situations when we were more impressionable than usual.

Who knows what had been going on with Olga from Russia, Allison from Britain or Paulien from South Africa? Or what might have happened with Maresol from Mexico or Adriana from Brazil? I wouldn't say that GJ was Snidely Whiplash, but he had a gift for sensing an opportunity when he needed it because he enjoyed—yes, enjoyed—and benefited from living vicariously through others' rich and satisfying lives.

I had to get some fresh air, so I headed outside to connect with my garden for a bit. I trimmed and savoured the smells from the hazelnut leaves then, after enjoying a sun massage through her fur, Dona carried off a few branches to use as her toothpicks. Because of my energy rationing, I could only do my trimming and weeding one wheelbarrow at a time. This seemed to describe how we women were stacking up the facts about GJ.

I headed inside to wash off and pour a mug of tea and link up with my new team. First of all, I wanted to express my deep gratitude for their agreement to go back to that hurt place within each one of them and to be once again off-balance while we discussed the out-of-order man. When on Skype late that Sunday morning (early evening, in Europe), I asked the ladies if I might talk about Caroline and GJ's mourning. There was a confused silence and equally baffled looks on their faces.

Walking on Heads

In synchronization, they each said, "He never had a fiancée who died!" It turns out that there never, ever had been a Caroline. At least, not one who had been killed in a crash! Barbra only knew that there had been a Caroline who was GJ's father's best friend's daughter and his Swiss summer companion from childhood. GJ had never had a Swiss girlfriend, never mind one who had breathed her last breath in a collision, and he had in no way had to deal with any heartbreaking loss that they knew of.

The room was spinning and I felt like I was falling into a vortex. I'm sure that my colour changed perceptibly. GJ had walked on my head—in fact, all of our heads—and as I cleared my mind of all the murmuring and chattering, I wished that I could hire an airplane and write in the sky over his present neighbourhood on Lake Ontario: 'BUGGER OFF GJ!'

He had inserted that story into my grief! I was at a loss for words and breathlessly continued listening to their discussions. My mind wandered, but I registered about a six on my Richter scale as they shared even more about his personal garbage.

Goos never finished his academic schooling, because he had spent his late teens in juvenile detention—maybe missing his chance at Caroline. The word through Barbra, as told to her by GJ's older sister, was that his childhood had been filled with anxiety and a fear of failing in their father's eyes. She hypothesized that this may have precipitated his habit of lying and using his choirboy looks to get his way. It was also possible that his sister was too young to appreciate that their father was profoundly afraid of and for his son, knowing that the golden boy had a stitch loose in him (or as we would say in English, was not wired right). Goos' father may have felt shame that he had produced a black seed. It's so heart-rending that the soul of the young Goos was damaged at such an undeveloped age.

At least he never got the Swiss girl. Lucky lass!

Both Barbra and Jana squealed that GJ had not graduated from university, did not have a job with the Dutch government and did not collect art. Even through their very different accents and their fast words, I recognized the truth. I heard their shock as well, as they cursed him for

All Together Now

his insensitivity in making up the dead fiancée story and for moving in on the loss of my precious child. That lie made me want to throw down the gauntlet and make him face the facts and look at his barren self, but I knew I would never, ever get a straight answer.

The details about his convoluted life crowded in on each other, filling us with renewed worry, paired with a passion to warn others about such broken people. With each of my new collaborators, GJ had not only portrayed himself as larger than life, but also served up anecdotes about how each woman who had come directly before her had been obsessive or jealous, which may explain Marie's response to Jana . . . and me. He claimed that every one, starting with Anne, had ruined his confidence in lasting relationships. He had also maintained they had each eventually hounded him to return to them. He claimed the pressure became unbearable and every time he had to move on.

We agreed that the truth was that the GJerk needed to weave insecurity and pathos into all of his relationships to extort attention and sympathy—for himself. The other truth was that Anne, at least, had escaped her baffling relationship with GJ and had found a bodyguard in a new partnership. She kept her distance and had never bothered to ask for support because of the fact that GJ had no job, income, stable address or residence in the Netherlands. Anne had a new life and family and wanted as little contact as possible with GJ or his escapades, including his victims.

12

The Droste Effect

> In the beginning is my end.
> — T.S. Eliot —

Since the shit hit the fan, I have done an enormous amount of introspection. I know, for example, how to use my vacuum cleaner and that it works by sucking up particles by some engineering feat of negative action—I do not grasp the physics. However, I did do a little studying up on that startling term 'sociopath'—not to know how it works or whether it is a design flaw that could be fixed, but just to become adjusted to the term and the real things these people did to other real people. I briefly joined a Facebook support group for those of us experiencing the fallout from locking lips with an imposter, because I just needed to know why some people are vacuums and why some of us get sucked up.

My plan was to remove the attachment I had to the invented parts of GJ. It was crazy to think that that the 'someone' whom I'd liked and loved had the scruples of a machine and the shape-shifting skills of an octopus.

I have gained some knowledge about ASPD, or Antisocial Personality Disorder—actually, more information that I wanted to have. There are numerous people on this planet like GJ whose behaviours are self-centred, who lack principles and scruples and thus a sense of guilt or genuine concern for others. Their attempts to appear to be sensitive can be baffling, because they cannot sustain emotional exchanges for long periods and their emotions may flip-flop, making others feel rapt and baffled at the same time.

The actions and logic of a person with ASPD are assembled in such a bizarre way that any—or more—of these terms and adjectives may fit what presents as bewildering behaviour: borderline personality disorder, social predator, sociopath, narcissist, charming predator, grandiose, pathological liar, guiltless, promiscuous, impulsive . . .

This disorder is essentially exhibited like the Droste effect, the art technique that portrays recursive images—a picture of someone holding the same picture showing the person holding the same picture. My opinion is that each lie told due to ASPD diminishes the fundamental person, with every attempt at mesmerizing others leading to the point where the genuine person is indistinguishable from the actor.

The pathology also reveals a similarity to the Droste art effect in that the camouflage or personas customized by those with ASPD are like the Droste effect's mathematical structure, teasing the victim's vision and expectations. The altered person does not reflect the true picture, but rather plays with the viewer's equilibrium, with many uncertain side effects.

One theory is that the emptiness of the person with ASPD can be the result of an inner play of genetics and environment, including emotional trauma or neglect from a primary caretaker. In order to survive, ASPD sufferers may learn early on to mimic the kind of child their caretakers want. Due to those pressures, they may abandon their authentic selves, inventing false personalities in order to escape failure. They can, consequently, become skilled at wearing masks resembling who we want them to be.

Another theory is that they simply have faulty wiring or a smaller frontal cortex in their brains than 'normal' people and some smaller areas within the amygdala (the centre for emotional activity) resulting in very shallow emotions and an inability to be 'real'. As a mother, teacher and fellow human, this makes me very sad for them.

It is complexly difficult to be more specific, because there is no cookie-cutter example of a person with ASPD, since each lies somewhere on a continuum from being a 'lite' enchanting liar (like the con artist in the book *Catch Me If You Can*) to a scary heavy-duty abuser. Nonetheless, I gather that what the psychologists call 'narcissistic injury' can escalate their wayward behaviour from relatively benign to unstable, which makes me so grateful that I had the sixth sense warning me not to push my man's buttons or to nag him for answers. The fact that Max had moved back in with me and the unusual phalanx of close friends that I had around me also possibly saved me from harm.

And—*quelle surprise!*—the common denominator amongst ASPD persons and their most outstanding characteristic is that the majority of them are well-liked. They are welcomed into society because of their charm and compelling charisma and as think-on-their-feet communicators. Like GJ, who was an accomplished mimic, most are smart, fascinating and exciting . . . until reality steps in and their behaviour is tested.

Dittoing that, many people with ASPD are narcissists, using others to fulfill what is called their 'narcissistic supply'. This is the term for what these parasites are obsessed with, which in GJ's case was respect and excitement. The appetite for this egotistic diet is ravenous, because narcissists are basically emotionally empty and have to dip into other people's feedbags, so to speak.

They need many partners or options at hand to gratify their hunger for constant stimulation and adoration. I was not alone in feeling so drained by the strange affair with my sociopath. Here is a reworded comment from one of my male support-group members:

> Anyone who is a target of a sociopath should be happy to know that all of us were chosen because we possess the positive character traits that they can never have . . . they

chose us because we made them appear to look like real, decent humans while they disembowelled our emotions and stole our souls...

People possessing ASPD traits are short on any kind of anxiety over their inconsiderate activities, unless their backs are to the wall and their personal safety, security or freedom at risk. ASPD sufferers feel that rules are for others, so if they are confronted about their tasteless actions, these charming predators can rationalize their activities, win over others with their charisma, redirect the blame and even make the blameless appear to be disturbed. These perpetrators bank on their victims' silence and the fact that we may be the ones to appear touched if we blow the whistle on them.

This is what makes it so crazy for the innocent.

Behind their masquerade, sociopaths usually don't ever even feel that they have psychological or emotional problems. Therefore, they see no reason to change their behaviour to conform to societal standards that they do not agree with. It is creepy, but trained professionals—including the police and psychologists—can often be fooled by their acts.

The most spine-chilling piece on the subject of pathological behaviour is simple but sinister and makes me gag. Dr. Robert Hare's team at the University of British Columbia explained that sociopaths have identical patterns when doing this to us, whether it's towards a person in the supermarket, a family member or a targeted victim. The first stage is identifying trusting spirits. The sociopath then reflects our valued personality traits back at us so we feel comfortable with them and think we should trust them. They also let us know that they like us. The next phase is the 'stage-managing' (or 'influencing') period, where we are drawn into their web by their use of fabricated stories that make them seem fascinating and safe. The last phase is the 'abandonment' period, where the sociopath makes plans to leave after we are of no more use or when we are onto them.

In a nutshell, sub-criminal antisocial personalities victimize others by operating in non-lethal ways by manipulating and misleading the

The Droste Effect

unsuspecting. They may use twisted logic, borrowed stories or phony promises, all in an attempt to disguise their shallow emotions and their sense of adequacy—in other words, they need supplements of healthy adaptive behaviours to appear healthy.

A Yup'ik Eskimo was asked by an anthropologist a few years ago what his culture would do with a man who repeatedly lied, cheated, stole and took sexual advantage of women. The reply was straightforward: somebody would have pushed him off the ice when nobody else was looking.

Hear that rumbling? It's me screaming at the utter devastation ASPD people leave in their wake. I was very lucky, yet I still feel the dizzy after-effects, knowing that GJ is not through with his lies. Still, I would not wish him to drown under an ice floe.

13
Everyone is a Citizen Journalist

In the long run, you hit only what you aim at. Therefore, though you should fail immediately, you had better aim at something high.
— Henry David Thoreau —

Some people must think that we women must have all been really, really gullible to be taken in by such a flawed guy. Let me put this out there: how can any of us tell if someone is lying or play-acting, especially when we ourselves don't live a lie? Do you think we can smell it a mile away? Is the con act obvious in the eyes or in the voice or in the body language? Do fakers drool or look up at flying saucers with a peculiar squint? Forgive the silliness, but sometimes it is obvious and we just know when someone or something is bogus. However, we don't always know that we don't know and those little or big fibs can get by any of us.

When someone feels the need to tell stories and has practiced playing roles minus the squints, the warble in the voice, and any glaring illogic or nonsense, it calls for intuition on high alert to detect any of the funny business. It is challenging to take resourceful, affirmative action, particularly when passion is in the mix! The truth may fall into place so very slowly that there can be a trail of people left wondering how they were duped until they look back and think, *I should have known . . .*

Walking on Heads

After GJ had been gone for several months, my dear brother Errki and his bromance partner Jonny had the cheek to joke, "We wondered if he was straight up or if he was blowin' smoke at you about the Africa thing." Fortunately, most of us get that anyone—that is you, me and the bourgeoisie—could be taken in by an extremely charming, smart narcissist and practiced liar. Stalin, Hitler and Pol Pot, as examples, escorted their entire nations into tyranny!

A part of me wonders if we are all somewhat desensitized to fake people because we live in a society of *faux* citizens. From beneath the rocket's red glare come a phalanx of beauty pageants, beginning with toddlers with fake hair, prosthetic eyelashes, spray tans and sexy attitudes. These shows and adverts are juxtaposed with peeps at rich-bitch housewives taunting us with their petty troubles. Then there is the rash of criminal shows on TV marching more counterfeit people and ways of life across the screen, followed by news about gang violence and drug wars. In our sucker society, the isolation from reality caused by many of our social media sources amps up the drama in our own lives so that we become numb to real-life performances. So, my point is that sociopaths can easily hide amongst all the other imitations in our culture.

Looking back on the pinball game that created this unusual sisterhood, I was so grateful that I was not alone in my light-headedness regarding our phoney dude. The others had worked through the guilt stage, which was a huge help to me in dealing with mine. I was at the point of feeling very apologetic for getting my daughter and friends involved in this drama and for giving away some of Max's inheritance. Everyone seemed to appreciate and relate to my guilt over being shaken up by GJ. My European friends also had studied the pathology and let me know, in no uncertain terms, that I was chosen for my grace, not for my flaws.

However, they could not help me with my personal experience of isolation. I was shy to meet colleagues or neighbours or acquaintances, who would wonder how I was handling my grief and how I was doing with my own health crisis and where GJ had got to. I avoided going

Everyone is a Citizen Journalist

back to my school or participating in social activities within my larger community network so that I wouldn't have to talk about Nathalie's death, my feelings, or the future. I couldn't even tell the men in my life. So, I turned to the group of nine other women.

I opened myself up as one who was feeling bruised and re-bruised every time I looked into someone's eyes and saw reflected back what I thought of as pity. Each woman reminded me that first of all, I got off fairly unscathed and, second, that I'd been extraordinary at dealing with the past year with all its insults so far. I just felt very self-conscious about carrying so much on my shoulders and consequently, I chose to spend more and more time in the sanctuary of my home, out of the spotlight.

We mostly talked about GJ and less about ourselves, but after the volleys of information-sharing done at net speed had finally settled down, Barbra suggested that we meet in the Netherlands and burn GJ's pictures. It was a sweet gesture, but of course I wouldn't ever be ready or able to fly again to do that.

Since it was impractical given our commitments and we never would find the energy or the time to flame his snapshots near his favourite canal, Barbra came up with a glam idea: we could burn Goos Dickensheets Jank on a blog instead. We agreed that we would walk and jump and stamp on him together and then, with a unified effort, we would vomit the phony from our lives.

First of all, I had never blogged. Second, I still cringed at the term 'sociopath', although all three of the others had read and researched it extensively after the shock of their joyride with twinkling blue-eyed GJ. *But he was very social and charming!* was one of my first thoughts about the scary word, like all sociopaths act and look like Freddy Krueger. Thank the Lord, I didn't share my naïveté publicly. Sorry to say, GJ's actions, deceptions, lies and manipulations actually were a bit reminiscent of Freddy, if you add an attractive face, a sexy voice, charm and boyish emotional innocence.

So, to make our sordid stories public, we decided to sing in astringent harmony on a blog. GJ would own the lowly moniker of 'Whatshisname'" and

Walking on Heads

we would each have our own pen names. It was all rather innocent of us to think that we could alter events, because despite the fact that each of us was well-educated and level-headed over most things, we were chosen for a particular innocence. Nevertheless, our blogging would show our stance against his disgusting and appalling behaviour, and it would be our collective purging to expose the 's'path' syndrome.

Since I was the most in need of a rebuild and because I had the free time and the best command of written English, I volunteered to do the deed. I felt that until my illness resolved itself, I would help to tell this story by standing up rather than being knocked over like a bowling pin. This would be part of my legacy for Max: to choose battles wisely and speak up with integrity and boldness! Civil disobedience can contain a subtle blend of moral high ground mixed with moderate blows of ricocheted words. Tit for tat.

This blogging thing was a steep learning curve for me, but I was given a break from chemo and my mind was clearing. The first thing that had to be done was to find a good blogging host. Then I needed to set up an account for us, locate a creative never-been-used name for it, think about my own nickname and figure out the design ins-and-outs of our site.

After another headache, one evening in early March while the traffic sounds were dying down outside my window, I became at one with the keyboard and launched our very own blog called Cruel Bastaard (the Dutch spelling of the word), which the women had all agreed was the perfect name . . . and was available!

It took a number of creative tries for an unused username, but I finally settled on my alias: 'Danced Upon'. The next step was a breeze, as I easily generated the "about" descriptor for cyber-readers:

> This site is about healing from the ordeal of coping with a pathological liar (one in particular), and his international victims.

Everyone is a Citizen Journalist

Eat crow, you fart, was my last thought before I fell asleep at my desk.

Later that night, after I massaged the kinks out of my back and neck and had a quick pee, I decided I could either close the blog site—which was still open under the screensaver—or I could post our first ever 'buzz'. My family says that I can be an Energizer bunny, so true to form, I got on it.

I love the clip-and-paste feature in word publishing. "The Undignified Tale of the Missing Wallet" was re-edited and published in full view of the computerized world. As Woody Allen said, "eighty percent of success is showing up." And even better, he once wisecracked that "Life doesn't imitate art, it imitates bad television." So here we would be, linked together by our own mind-blowing series.

I would love to say that it felt good to post my first offering, but instead it felt oddly nasty and disloyal—until I remembered that we were with the good guys. While I was still trying to wrap my head around the terms 'sociopath', 'antisocial personality' and even 'narcissist', I kept thinking *When you get to the end of your rope, tie a knot and swing like a Cirque du Soleil performer*. We were the ones reclaiming our reason, sanity and exploited selves. We had something worth producing. We would be crocheting our souls into a performance that would shout "*Merde!*"

March 4, 2011   Posts: 1
This could be a classic fable about an   Views: 22
inheritance snatcher, or a parable about a
vulnerable woman, or the account of the
truths and consequences of that esteemed
quality called trust. But we'll just call it: *The
Undignified Tale of the Missing Wallet*

Once upon a time, two people met at a market in the western Canadian provinces. Whatshisname was a tall, charming and mesmerizing Dutchman and she, a willowy Canadian woman. Across the space swished the dashing Dutchman in his Italian boots. As they chatted, they shared those parts that people often do when meeting: their pedigrees. She was a school teacher entrusted with children's minds, and he was in Canada as a representative of the Netherlands Ministry of Foreign Affairs. Or so the tale goes ...

The Dutchman and the equally tall and stylish Canadian danced into each other's lives for that afternoon and for many days and nights to follow. Three months into this brilliant relationship, the Canadian woman sensed that the man needed to return to his homeland. He offered to take her back with him, but because she was a mother with an ailing child, she chose to stay behind in Canada.

A year later, just before Michaelmas, Whatshisname reconnected with the woman, because as it turned out, he never had left Canada at all. The skeleton the Dutchman was hiding in the cupboard was an on-and-off domestic relationship with another Canadian woman.

How appreciative the younger Canadian woman was to have the beguiling Dutchman return from abroad (or so she thought) to desire her again, especially during troubled times! Before long, he moved in to support her through the grief over the death of her daughter. He was welcomed into the Canadian's circle of family and friends, who were all grateful for his cooperation and protection.

But along with his charm and kindness loomed an interesting piece of fiction. The tall tale was that the man had no wallet, only border-crossing papers. His wallet (or so the story goes) had been left in his topcoat in the other Canadian lady's carriage.

So life with the new Canadian carried on, until his grieving partner asked about his ongoing lack of money. Not even a penny did he ever carry! Whatshisname claimed his ex-lady would send the wallet; then claimed that he had cancelled his important documents, then said that his banker in Holland would dispatch funds.

For six long months, the Dutchman maintained that his solvency was near and that he would look after his financial obligations, but would first require a small loan to travel home to get his affairs in order in person.

Whatshisname left Canada again and carried on with letters for three months, describing his work in Africa and his dimwitted Dutch accounting firm and how discouraged he was. He claimed that he and the money would return in good time.

On the morning of the first day of spring, the younger Canadian woman received a letter from a woman named Whatshername from Toronto. It said briefly that Whatshisname had been living with her again since the fall and that had agreed to stay there.

There had been no journey overseas, no financial negotiations and no intention to repay the loan or his part in living well in British Columbia. The younger maiden was simply given a statement that she had been passed by for the other woman.

Love can be messy and unkind, but not a runaway misdeed. So, the west coast girl wrote back to the other woman informing her of the unpaid debts of her lover, but the letter was returned.

Undignified—indeed!

Tags: *thief, liar, misrepresentation, cheating*
Categories: *used and abused, pathological lying, international romance scam*

Comment from Ajuoga (Annelies): I am one of the Dutch women he manipulated and cheated. His 'art' of lying is his 'success story' because without education, work and incomes he has been managing to live in comfort for many, many years, using love, friendship and friends of friends. He assumes correctly, that nobody will check his fabricated stories about his private life and his fictitious professional work, and those who might try to screen him get to nowhere, because there are no traces behind him. Holland was too small for his games. He tried in other countries as well, but Canada has opened the best opportunities—so far from Europe and his real identity cannot be checked because he has been unregistered from his homeland! He can get more fame abroad, feed his vanity and narcissism—GJ the Conqueror! He knows how to impress and deceive both men and women, regardless of the age. What his next achievement will be? Will he stay with M in Toronto?? or will move to N, or O or P woman (in China? Africa?). There are many victims who will believe his words, his lying eyes, will protect him in the name of love, giving him shelter, food, clothes and shared beds. New friends will give a helpful hand to introduce him to their friends. His vicious circle will grow, his web is strong. If people were less naive and ready to check strangers like GJ, he would be a beggar under a bridge.

Comment from Circe (Barbra): For sure you will not get any money back, there is no civil law to prosecute him because he has no job, lives without permanent address and he knows rules and regulations to protect himself. You know he is a psychopathic liar and a genius in that 'job'. You will not win, it is better to forget the pain and humiliation and use your energy in a positive way. He never loved you nor any other woman. He uses 'love' to deceive and get existential profits for himself. Whatshername made a big mistake not to warn you but to support and take back the freak instead. Quite cruel. You should demand from her clear answers about the jerk.

Comment from Fobo (Ev): How do you say Asshole in Dutch?

Everyone is a Citizen Journalist

Comment from Big Fish (Jana): WhatsHERname evidently took her story with GJ as in the last verses of "Nights in White Satin" (extended version): "Cold hearted orb, that rules the night, removes the colours, from our sight, Red is gray and Yellow white, But we decide, which is right and Which is an Illusion."

Comment from Dancedupon: Thank you Moody Blues for these poignant words.

14

A Real Man Never Hits a Woman

*If we did all the things we are capable of,
we would astound ourselves.*

— Thomas Edison —

Posting "The Undignified Tale of the Missing Wallet" was only a taste of what was to come. Our sisterhood had the unblemished genetics which allowed us to be cooperative team players. We were evolved and he was not, so as a force to be reckoned with, I put up two more blog posts within the week. We wanted our readers (should there ever be any) to get a fuller picture of the erroneousness that was the lifestyle of GJ and others like him. We needed to lean on each other and electronically shout "Hell, yeah!" once we had him pegged through our blogging.

The Canada geese were back, honking their way through the sky on their northern journey, so I continued the blogging expedition with "All that Glitters is not Gold," which I posted the next day. We had collectively decided to slowly depict ASPD through a real illustration of the pattern and how it affected us real women. We were on a blogging roll, ready to go public and comment on his immorality!

Walking on Heads

March 8, 2011
All that Glitters is not Gold

Posts: 2
Views: 53

I never, ever thought that I would be writing about something like this, especially as the 'collateral damage' of a half-man.

'Vulnerable' is not my middle name, but a mammoth weight had landed on my heart during and after my daughter's illness and death. I was supported and loved—if a sociopath can indeed love—by a nice-looking and (I was led on to think) scrupulous Dutchman. This man showed up when I needed strong shoulders and he let me lean on him for emotional comfort. In return, he leaned on me for shelter and money; not as part of an agreement, but by being economical with the truth.

After he abruptly left because I asked him to man-up financially, I discovered that I was not the only casualty of his charms. When emptying my space of his things, I found receipts that would lead me to three other women in Europe who had been deceived by this guy.

Perhaps for the sake of his own assumed roles, he chooses smart, successful, attractive and special women to disguise the fact that he himself is not scholarly, prosperous, pleasant or distinctive, except as a cad and a liar.

The details of Whatshisname's half-truths revealed by his other victims are sometimes appalling, often disgusting and absurdly bold, reflective of an illusive mind.

This has led me to open this blog for us Amazons to highlight the fact that there are devils of all ages among us!

Tags: used and abused, liar
Categories: sociopath, liar, immoral

A Real Man Never Hits a Woman

Comment from Circe (Barbra): This mockingbird is rotten from inside and his outer shell losing gloss. By getting older, his mimicry will slowly break him down because he is also a cheater on himself. One day, he will be confused with who he really is. HE CAN CONTACT US FOR HIS LOST IDENTITY!

New vulnerable ladybirds use internet and networking—difficult time is coming for the mimicking bird because he cannot hide himself behind the web much longer. I sometimes pity him and his gloomy future, but that no-empathy-bird does not know what I mean. No one can help him to re-socialize because he has fake wings.

Do not feel upset, Danced Upon. Be relieved you could get rid of him (as it is not always easy). Now you need time to clean your hurt feelings and you have so many persons around to support you in this process.

Comment from Big Fish (Jana): How is he such a good liar? He smartly uses the few things he has learnt from his numerous women: Circe and I discovered so many stories he had narrated around which were either our personal or his friends' experiences ... not his!

Refusing strongly his own personality (frankly, I don't blame him for this), he needs other persons' characters, so he learnt how to change roles easily, by putting on a new mask, entering into new personalities to drag people into his traps, with special emphasis on using 'feelings'.

I remember how often he stirred me up to talk about my feelings, how often he required me to analyze with him the behaviour and feelings of other persons ... He is an incredible actor but very bad as a 'scriptwriter', because he cannot catch the dynamic aspects of human relations (consequently he cannot foresee them either). There is always something arrogant and narcissistic about all the personalities he interprets. As a thief who had stolen our parts, he is triumphantly proud of how he 'assembled' all those fragments. But, vice versa, these thefts are serving only his 'Ego', hidden behind all these personalities. Greedy for 'Superiority', he needs people he admires to feed that Bestial Avid Ego. That Beast doesn't understand at all that human feelings are REAL, not FICTIVE as his.

15

Six Foot Two, Eyes of Blue

They can because they think they can.
— Virgil —

Whatshisname had left behind more than a few items at my Vancouver abode. He also left a trail leading to the other ladies who had shared their open hearts, trust and moments of vulnerability with Whatshisname when he stepped into their lives. We all had experienced the charm, the fascination of his career and contacts, his fictitious love of his children and his connection with our circles of families and friends. We all had been walked upon and left without payment for the loans he received from each of us. Lost wallets were sometimes misplaced, cards or lost baggage gone astray, or a death in the family required a sudden departure. Each story begged for sympathy and concern.

The absolute beauty of our new sisterhood was that women as a sex are often innately cooperative—at least we have evolved that way, because we need groups or packs to defend ourselves against predators, we need cooperatives to make communal living comfortable and frankly, we need the company of others. Thus, our sisterhood had a common bond and a familiar means of communication, support and genuine concern and caring. We all had to cope with GJ's heartless duplicity.

Walking on Heads

I had not confided in my brother Paul, Jack or Richard. In fact, I couldn't bring myself to tell any of them at first. Richard was the first to hear about my situation. I guess I will never know why, but I have not heard from him since I disclosed what GJ had done. I texted him once but he did not reply.

Annelies talked with GJ's sons as well as his sister about our blog. Only Michiel showed any interest, which was understandable, but none of us of were brought into the picture as to his thoughts. That was fine with us because we didn't want to involve any of the children, including our own, for fear of traumatizing them more.

I did, however, send a note to GJ's friend Arne, giving him an update on the pieces that were falling into place.

> Thank you, Arne, for your kind reply last month.
>
> I often referred to GJ as a man-boy, which I think is also how you may see him. I'm glad that you love him and that he has a steadfast friend like you.
>
> He has, indeed, been in Toronto for five months while claiming to me that he was working hard in Tanzania, although Canada Borders and Crossings has since enlightened me that GJ has not left our country in months and is in overstay of his visa. I think he's kept in touch so that he would have the option of returning, although as it turns out, he's also been sending love notes to Jana hoping to return to her, perhaps when he or Marie tire of one another again.
>
> You see, I found a receipt in the GPS case that GJ left here. It was for Jana's payment for his cellphone and so I was able to connect with Jana, Annelies and Barbra. These ladies, amongst others, have been deeply hurt in

numerous ways by your friend and I'm afraid that we four are going public with our stories. I'm so sorry but we feel that others need to be warned about this type of person. Did you know that Goos claimed to have a Swiss fiancée, Caroline, who died in a car crash, and that he used that pathos to counter the loss of my daughter? Did you know that he portrayed himself as a Ph.D working for the Dutch government, which I suspect your government may not be too happy about? Did you know that he pinched money from a charity he started in the Balkans?

I could ask many more questions and give various twisted details that I have learned from his past conquests, but I'll stop. A part of me finds it fascinating that your friend can put on a persona like a new set of clothes. Fascinating and simultaneously repellent! Thank you again for the extra clarity you have brought to this story. My heart actually goes out to him in some strange way but I know that I am well rid of his pathology.

Regards,
Anni

Understandably, I never received a response and I figure that I was not the first lady that Arne realized had been duped by his friend. And so, I wrote the next blog post as a personal exploration of what we women had faced because we had welcomed someone so intimately into our lives.

Memories of the good times, or of who we had thought was a first-class man with a beguiling story, occasionally resurfaced. However, we each knew intellectually that his persona reflected the traits and characteristics we valued in ourselves, not the artificial man.

Walking on Heads

March 12, 2011
Killing us Softly

Posts: 3
Views: 98

Exposing the fraud that is the lifestyle of GJ Whatshisname is bittersweet. This pathological liar who crossed so many hearts is eventually going to trip up and will meet his match. He will be made accountable to authorities one day.

But he is not evil.

That's where the conundrum lies. Because we are ethical, nurturing, thoughtful and emotional women, it's awkward to take action against someone else, to even delve into the stories that reveal that this significant person in our lives was a fraud. To write about it is partially healing and partially intensely stressful. To know that one day he will be stopped and made accountable is also gruelling.

It is not black and white for us. We grapple with our consciences and love for this man. We have love for him because he is a man-boy, because he has a mental illness and if nothing else, because he replenishes the environment by breathing out compounds for the plants.

We believe that there is a part of him desperately wanting to be someone worthy of respect.

We are not in love with him anymore! In truth, a part of us despises him for posing as someone he is not. We are disgusted that he has hurt children with his lies and that he exploited our trust, our friends, our bank accounts and our health. We recommend that he take a seminar to delete his limiting beliefs about his authentic self.

We recognize and understand that we are responsible for our own reactions to situations. We, and no one else, can choose to dwell on the rat's nest that he left behind in our hearts. As Anne Frank wrote, "In spite of everything I still

Six Foot Two, Eyes of Blue

believe that people are really good at heart. I simply can't build up my hopes on a foundation consisting of confusion, misery and death."

Even though at this point in our process it feels like it is killing us softly, we are supporting each other through our recovery, knowing that karma will eventually be our knight in shining armour.

Tags: exploiting of trust
Categories: liar, antisocial personality disorder

Comment from Duped (my girlfriend, Liz): My husband and myself were completely taken in by GJ. He charmed us a number of times with his work anecdotes and his travels throughout the world. We were fascinated by his libertarian heart and were willing to chant for the orange team with him at the Richmond Oval during the Winter Olympic Games. We were above all in high spirits for 'Danced Upon' after all she had been through in the last couple of years. But when she told us about his defrauding her of her kindness and ignoring her requests for her money, we were sickened. What a cold-hearted performance he put on and for that we consider him a very, very sad human being!

16

Raise a Little Hell

What kind of world would it be if everyone in it were just like me?
— Antoine de Saint-Exupéry —

Frankly, my dear, I didn't give a damn that people might recognize GJ from the blog. Correction: I did give a damn and wondered how I could be so nasty. He was basically kind with me, I thought, as the good parts came flooding back. My memories of the pleasant GJ and those of the lying GJ were somehow detached, but his successive secrets and lies were my confirmation that he was as flimsy as a paper doll cut-out.

I did give a damn that he had fleeced my bank account, that he had pulled the wool over my eyes and that, worse than that, he had promised my friends he was caring for me and my family through our heartbreak. Barbra and my friend Linsey pantomimed on Skype that he was a loser (the thumb/forefinger 'L' gesture) and regurgitated that his type needed to be stopped. Inside, I was gleefully thinking to myself, *GJ, you thought I was a pushover and too tired to contend with you!*

As Pierre Trudeau once said, when dramatic action was needed during the crisis in Quebec in 1970 and he invoked the *War Measures Act*: "Just watch me!" I would be more than white noise as I linked arms together with the other women, paying homage to the goddesses of truth on our modern day altar of words.

March 12, 2011   Posts: 4
Wie is GJ Whatshisname?   Views: 163

There is an English idiom: 'Put your money where your mouth is.' Translated, this means that a person should back up words with action.

Who is this man, GJ Whatshisname? Is it okay to slot him under the category of a professional liar? Does he ever follow through on his promises? Is he a moral idiot and a hypocrite? Or is he a well-meaning man whose soul jumped ship ages ago?

I struggle with labels and name-calling, which are counter to my nature and to my values. However, it was and still can be difficult to digest the fact that GJ's behaviour can be . . . off. GJ (a.k.a. Whatshisname) is not a degenerate man. But he is not a decent one either. With a friendly, trustworthy shtick, he chooses to borrow occupations, time, money, shelter, reputations and some of our futures without our consent.

The evidence is that GJ creates fantastical stories so that he can insert himself into others' respectable lives. There seem to be some consistencies in how he does this. Whatshisname is drawn to intelligent women who are productive and established in their careers. He is attracted to women who are fit and appealing and solvent. And he gives few reasons for them to distrust that he is not just the same.

One might wonder whether GJ Whatshisname really knows that it's wrong to be supported by another without their approval or consent. The anemic phrase 'to put your money where your mouth is' proves to be a one-sided deal with this Dutchman!

Raise a Little Hell

Tags: put your money where your mouth is!
Categories: liar, scammer, thief

Comment from Circe (Barbra): OUR little gangster is 'cute' and 'smart', so he thinks. But he is not! He believes he is superior or BETTER because even people with university degrees and high positions fall into his social traps and love his funny way to be. To discover who he really is, contact previous victims to compare stories!

GJ repeats the same tricks and the same personal, family and vocational tales. I, Ajuoga and Big Fish compared his lies, his e-mails, his letters and the stories he told to each of us and we became forever friends—the good thing we got from the jerk. We have all agreed that liars have a mixer in their heads—if you start asking them questions they get muddled and spray nonsense.

17

Hero or Villain?

It is only with the heart that one can see rightly; what is essential is invisible to the eye.
— Brian Tracy —

We were picking up speed in our indignation. None of us were heated with romantic fury, but we were grateful to be out of his sphere of dishonesty and duplicity. He had passed his expiry date with each of us, as things had soured though his conduct.

We were purging his deceit by airing the details to each other. Comments and information were flying though the cyber-web as we toasted to our union. The blog posts were almost benign compared to the things Jana or Barbra or Annelies disclosed to me and my friends, and in contrast to the clashes we were starting to experience with each other due to the anxieties that we were all re-experiencing. Without telling my daughter much about my whirlwind existence, I carried on like a duck: I was calm on the surface but my little feet were paddling under the water very briskly. It would be months before I would debrief Maxine with a condensed version of the reality of being taken in by GJ. She was still frozen by the losses of both Nat and Liana and she didn't need to know how shocked I was by his callous departure, although it may have given her an avenue for her anger. In retrospect, I just didn't want anything more to fan the flames of her sadness and her struggle over the unfairness of life.

The blog postings that were keeping my fingers and brain active were not nearly as riveting as the discussions and comments that followed. The blogs were the tease and the comments the taunt.

There was a huge chance that GJ would be furious with me, because he had been tame and obliging while staying in Vancouver and most likely believed his own fantasy that he'd been doing me a kindness. He had been decent with me . . . until he strung me up with his fictional money and travel lies. With any luck, he would be shocked by my stance and the public exposure that I was spearheading. The blog postings were pasting him into search engines along with his photos and we were delirious with excitement and wonderment. I was the picador who was doing the baiting and lancing. Since anger management is not a bull's strong suit, we were convinced that GJ was soon going to show his true colours and come charging back at us, nostrils flaring.

March 15, 2011   Posts: 5
Hero, or Villain?   Views: 239
(public photo from GJ's Facebook page)

There are times when it is still incomprehensible that I shared my home and lived with a pathological liar. I continue to have a hard time aligning the person I thought I knew with the person I am learning about through the women he was with before me. GJ was my shield, which is as close to a hero as I have ever had. He seemed to be sensitive to my emotional rollercoaster, and he was very thoughtful and helpful for the first three to four months of our partnership. My friends (including my exes) liked him and we were all grateful that I had help and a new love during the difficult time after the death of my eldest child.

Hero or Villain?

He was good company, funny and gentle. I think he enjoyed being a hero and an angel, as many of my friends referred to him then. He was captivating and smart... yet more and more arrogant as he compared Canada to Europe and ranted about fraudulent bankers, politicians and rich people in the U.S.

He figured that he could justify staying with me free of charge because he had promised to take me to Greece and then to Turkey. He said that he had his Italian car in storage there. Turns out his car had been forfeited years before for debts he had incurred in Europe.

With the lost wallet fiction, the hero sparkle started to dull. And ironically, he had a pale resemblance to some of the politicians and corporate leaders he disliked for their successes and obligations.

At what point did GJ start to morph into a dud in our relationship? It most certainly was related to the money talk, as he kept making excuses for not getting access to his euros or new credit cards. His lack of empathy for my own financial crisis was stunning!

The villain began to emerge, as his lack of follow-through with money and his story about leaving for a short work trip in Europe began to take shape. Still he was not entirely a villain in my eyes, but certainly a puzzle and a contradiction. And the worst part was, I couldn't talk to anyone about it—at first—because it was embarrassing to tell on a partner.

The crook flew his flag when he created a story about being away in Europe, then in Africa for two, then three, then almost four months. His narrative about working overseas was all an illusion to take the pressure off his debts and lies to me. It was crazy-making!

Villains stomp on our heads, making us doubt our sanity and our judgment, and they trample our trust.

Walking on Heads

This has been hard to admit, but GJ Whatshisname is a cruel bastard, *een harteloss bastaard,* lower on the evolutionary tree than a skunk. (Sorry to all skunks, who only get foul in response to danger.) Someone should Photoshop a stripe on his back!

Tags: cruel bastard, dud, skunk
Categories: pathological liars, villains

Comment from Zele (my girlfriend, Bryn): Like many people in our community, my husband and I were taken in by GJ's charismatic, friendly personality, and by the sensitive, gentle, caring way he had of taking care of our friend, who was so recently bereaved. There had been small signs, problems that needed to be resolved, and our friend and I attempted to problem-solve them when he was away. I always said what I thought openly as did she; at no time was there a 'burying of heads in the sand'.

After we found out just how disgustingly deceitful GJ had been, both my husband and I thought "I should have known." But we had no frame of reference for dealing with a person with a character like this. And we prefer to think the best of people, to give them the benefit of the doubt. We had tried, with increasing difficulty, to see the upside of what he was offering our friend in terms of emotional support and intellectual stimulation.

Now we are all left here, a bit shell-shocked, to process what happened and support our friend through her personal process.

Here is an e-mail I received from GJ, near the end of what he pretended was his "four-month trip to east Africa." It was in response to a query I sent him wondering how things were going on the other side of the world:

"In Stone Town, Zanzibar, again. Doing the round-trip with my newly appointed cohort. Should be finished in the next couple of weeks. Then I can finally return to British Columbia. It has been dragging on for a whole score of reasons. The basic one being that I am in the service of the NL Foreign Ministry and they want me to wrap up things here orderly. Deeply sorry I could not be back any earlier. Warmest regards to Lee and you, GJ"

Comment (from Duped): Hypocrisy is another variety of cruelty. Who was, or for that matter, who is this man? And do we actually care about him anymore?

Comment Linsey (a girlfriend of mine): Zele expresses the dilemma I felt about GJ ... we wanted to believe the best ... I wanted my dear friend to have a new love in her life. I wanted her to receive the help and comfort we all thought he was sincerely offering her. I wanted to support her and her choice in a man... I trusted her judgment even when my instincts sometimes said, "Are you sure he is for real??" ... Sadly GJ was not ... BUT what is for real is her friends love, support and appreciation of her exceptional courage and her unabashed humanity.

Comment from Fobo (from my cousin Ev): The man is an empty shell without an apparent soul. He is either truly insane or the devil incarnate, if there is such a thing. A loathsome individual, a lowly, conniving parasite feeding on his unsuspecting 'hostess' and her friends and family, the man is as far from redemption as the outer reaches of the universe. In short ... he's a piece of work, but not worth the effort.

Here we were, starting to feel empowered by telling our story with witnesses. It was my cousin, who is married to a lawyer, who had said, "He's a scumbag, Anni. Name him and use his photos. He's flying under

Walking on Heads

the radar and his next target just might search online, to check him out. Do it! Do it! Do it! He has no real reputation to ruin, only a trail of casualties, most of whom you'll never know."

I was doing more behind the scenes than just writing and talking with my 'sisters'. I was still a mom and I was even keeping the garden and my health together. I had also managed to be proactive and practical as I got down to the business of GJ, the offender. By the light of the silvery moon that still lit my spirit, I contacted the Canadian Anti-Fraud Line to register a complaint about GJ, for the record. They told me about a romance scam website. He hadn't stolen my name or my passwords as far as I knew, but I needed to tell someone that he had swindled me. Plus, I called the RCMP and was told that my grudge was a civil matter and that I needed evidence, but I could try to sue him.

I next took a stab at connecting with the NL Consulate, which at first registered my comments that GJ was posing as a representative of their government as significant, but a few days later I was told their hands were tied unless I pressed charges in Canada. This was stunning, because I couldn't charge him with posing as a socialist.

So before I ran out of steam, I called the Canada Border Services Agency, where the details were finally taken seriously—partly because I had a scanned a copy of his passport, which Jana had sent to me. At first it felt like an undercover operation, having a record of his passport, but it turned out to be another break for the good guys. GJ was, in fact, on overstay and I was assured that the information would be passed on to the Ontario authorities.

Except for the three single European women who liked knowing where he was, my friends and I hoped that GJ would be deported from Canada. Marie could keep him forever as far as those three were concerned. I knew that Marie would eventually return to my province, however, and that was too close for my comfort.

Meanwhile, I kept wrapping my words around the wings of our blog and the team kept responding.

Hero or Villain?

March 18, 2011
Goos Jank is the Great Pretender
(photo taken by Jana in Italy)

Posts: 6
Views: 315

Sincere apologies are offered to all the other men in the world also named Goos Jank. These men simply share the name, not the dark side of the man called worse things than a pretender by all the women he has hurt. The other men and boys named Goos Jank share a name discredited by this one, who hurts others in his posing as a wholesome, solvent man. But that is all they share. The opinions in the *Cruel Bastaard* blog represent the women who have been heartlessly and methodically used by the one and only Goos Dickensheets Jank, who was born in Rotterdam on February 26th, 1955.

The sad thing about our 'pretender' is that this man has a high degree of mental intelligence but a low degree of emotional aptitude. He does indeed present himself with people skills and was undoubtedly well-schooled as a child and adolescent. He speaks, reads and writes several languages with ease. He offers up charm, sophistication and seamless leadership. On top of that, he is a gifted storyteller.

The disgrace and sorrow is that this man had so much potential to actually be the man he pretends to be. He could have done so much that was good and productive and purposeful. GJ might even have had satisfying work as a translator or a motivational speaker.

But late bloomer GJ is lazy, antsy and plays the sympathy card when he needs things to go his way. He loves to be a nomad, moving internationally from woman to woman. He seems to get a high from fibbing about his finances, his children and former girlfriends; or at least, he needs to carry on the disguise because he is a no one.

Walking on Heads

The last couple of months he was at my home, he was supposedly 'working' on my computer doing 'research.' The smooth operator was also stalking an ex-girlfriend and reconnecting with another, who has since taken him back. And his response when I found him out was "I fucked up," said in a sheepish, charming way like a little boy with his hand caught in his pants ... I mean ... the cookie jar.

GJ is a FUCKUP who has crossed the wrong hearts!

Tags: thief, bastard, liar
Categories: sociopath, romance scammer

Comment from Broken Hallelujah (my friend, Nancy): You are an amazing writer, Danced Upon—and not so 'sweet', finally! Any luck on the RCMP front?

18

GJ is a Trompe l'Oeil

Life shrinks or expands in proportion to one's courage.

— Anaïs Nin —

At this point, it felt like we didn't have a lot to lose and that we had a calling. We weren't just sharing recipes, we wanted to plaster him across search engines and warn others about takers and fakers like him. We all agreed that if we had known about him or been able to find something about him, we would have laughed in his face as he tried his illusions with us. So our mission became to warn others, as well as to support each other in removing the weight of him from our lives.

I was aghast at the beastly ways in which he had used his sons. Annelies told me on Skype that once when the boys had competed in a soccer match in the north of Holland, GJ had told them to tell their coach that they had been mugged. They were to say that all of their travel money was gone.

She also said that one evening, when she was almost finished work at the hospital, GJ had sat in the courtyard waiting for her. A nurse whom Annelies knew well told her that a guy who she thought was GJ had talked her up during her break, telling her about his daughter who was upstairs recovering from a boating accident.

Walking on Heads

And, *la pièce de résistance* from the mouth of Annelies was that GJ had only lived with her for one year (not ten!) because she figured him out as parasite (as she called him). She eventually needed to have him escorted out of her life by some friends.

March 23, 2011   Posts: 7
Trompe l'Oeil literally translates from French   Views: 402
to mean 'fool the eye'. It is a visual illusion in
art, used to trick the eye into perceiving a
painted detail as a three-dimensional object.

It is interesting how we can name pedophiles and rapists as the criminals they are but cannot name the soft criminals who take our trust, our money and our faith in the inherent goodness of our fellow Earth-dwellers.

There are some among us who have no conscience, have charismatic qualities that seduce others with accomplished abilities to weave deceptively believable stories and personas.

There are sociopaths among us like ugly fungi: they taste good when served with other decent victuals, but depend on our perception of them being based on our own healthy values, morals, ethics and standards.

Pathological lying is as it sounds. It's a hard-wired disorder called moral idiocy, where a person has frontal temporal dementia in the areas of the brain that govern knowing right from wrong. These are liars who base their entire existence on glibly creating fantastic stories that get better as they perfect their 'gift'.

One of these people is Goos Jank. He travels internationally from woman to woman enjoying the good life without ever working or revealing his true self. He is charming, easygoing, attractive to both men and women ... but he is a time bomb with a set of beautiful blue eyes.

GJ is a Trompe l'Oeil

Sociopaths and liars should have 'WARNING' signs tattooed on their foreheads. Instead, people like GJ show us different sides of themselves when we either get too close or when we stand back too far. The midpoint is the dizziest place to stand and the only thing to do is run!

Tags: warning, fools the eye
Categories: sociopath, liar

Comment from Big Fish (Jana): When I met him at my cousin's home in Braga, he was shining joy, cordiality and a picture of a 'nice man'. He said he was in-charge as an employee of the Society of International Development Netherlands (completely false), he was a father of five children: three daughters from his previous marriage ('Circe' never married him or bore his children) and two with his actual wife with whom he had been married for twenty-two years ... well, that number was really a fantasy! Told with the only purpose to present him as skilful, to "manage everything in a joyful way" and to be liked—that's obvious.

As our friendship continued and transformed into a love-relationship, it inevitably involved the woman in NL, 'Circe', whom I thought was his wife and mother of his children, while in reality she was continuously deceived by his other false stories (beside the falsification of her signature in order to get the residence at her place as to renew his visa at the time). Later on, the stories inevitably involved his sons, too.

That would have been the point in which any person with some conscience would have pulled the brakes and stopped bullshitting. But not him! As his sons didn't want to deal with him at all, he explained their behaviour to me as their 'devotion' to their 'mother' and 'step-sisters'.

Walking on Heads

'Danced Upon' put a photo with the story "The Great Pretender" I shot of him in Rovereto, Italy, when we were on holiday at my expense. The photo on "Hero or Villain?" which he flaunts on Facebook, instead was shot by the woman who had 'imported' that human waste to Vancouver, Canada, and who re-took him again in Toronto. That photo was sent to me a few months after I kicked him out accompanying a letter full of love-feeling statements to me. I warned the woman he was a sociopath and prayed for her to warn every other. He sickens me with his pretended 'kindness' and 'worthiness', testifying only to his DECEPTION, of his cheating and manipulation which doesn't spare children. It testifies to the fact his disastrous life cruelly involves innocent persons, because it is not only his 'life', but his chosen way-of-living. This thing must stop, in one way or another. The society must find a manner to PROTECT itself from anti-social behaviours, because isolated individuals can't cope with the problem, which is the basic purpose of this blog!

Comment from Big Fish (Jana): 'Danced Upon' has forgotten his greatest 'professional' skill: his persuasion/dissuasion capacity he developed thanks to the fact he lives his whole his life through cheating, acting and pretending to be a 'sensible man' (excellently hiding the fact he was just a squeezing prostitute). He pretends at being a 'philosopher'... using his small (internet) knowledge and great experience with women, reflected in his acting their thinking, their stories, their characters and their skills. Indeed, there's something devilish in that use of other persons' traits which transforms into a sort of 'power' for him. He is so convincing because he interprets the emotions, thoughts and life experiences of the sensible and skilful women he has been with. So, the truth is we were all attracted by something which belonged to his former women and felt we

GJ is a Trompe l'Oeil

could struggle easier the obstacles of life with such a person nearby. But reality requires concrete contributions. It doesn't allow forever-actings . . . from the 'devil' who steals others goodness. If there's any positive lesson to be learnt from this: GJ's legacy is a living proof: women can struggle better when they unite their sensibility and skills.

* ☆ *

March 26, 2011   Posts: 8
I Will Gladly Pay You Tuesday for   Views: 490
a Hamburger Today
(photo caption 'Goos Dickensheets Jank')

How can it be legal to be a liar or a thief or a cruel bastard? At what point does a soft criminal become a hardened one?

For ages, philosophers have debated the morality of cheating, lying and stealing. Lawyers argue legal points, but as far as I can grasp, character, proper behaviour and ethics are left for kitchen-table disputes.

Our laws of the land are in place to prosecute predators who cheat, lie, steal or physically harm, injure or threaten others.

But the law needs evidence.

In the case of those who steal right from under our noses, sometimes we have no proof because even though we didn't give them permission to swindle us, the larceny may not leave a paper trail.

When someone assures us "I'll pay you back next week" or "The money is in the mail," these are only empty words without evidence that there was ever a loan or a receipt of favours. There are no grounds for a request for a payback from your 'friend'. There may be no witnesses to the intention to repay what was meant to be a loan as opposed to a handout.

In the eyes of the law it is pretty straightforward. The qualities of honesty and integrity do not seem to be legal terms. On the flipside, to be elusive or to be a knave of hearts has few, if any, legal repercussions. "Watch me pull a rabbit out of my hat ... oops, wrong hat!" is not punishable.

So, people like the Goos Janks of this world get away with living underground without paying the services of companies or reimbursing our governments' infrastructures with tax contributions; in fact, with no records of them as billable or taxable citizens at all. Nevertheless, the fallout from the deceptions and funds cadged is enormously tangible for the direct casualties of these leeches. We may have our purses drained and our minds twisted by lies upon lies that make no sense. Our trust may be damaged and our children traumatized, but most of all, the loss of our belief in right and wrong and the law being there to protect us can be the most personal injury.

Tags: thief, immorality
Categories: pathological lying

Comment from Big Fish (Jana): A proverb says: "The occasion makes the man a thief." I detested that popular wisdom so much that I ignored it and more than once in my life I showed a trust which brought me to important losses of my funds difficult to prove in front of justice. But at least I've learnt that it's possible to appreciate a general wisdom, without applying it personally. But nothing is so black. If Al Capone finished in prison for tax-evasion ... everybody can be 'hit' in unexpected ways. Even GJ! It will give little satisfaction to the victims of his frauds, but let's be modest and remember the exultation of Al

GJ is a Trompe l'Oeil

Capone's victims (not only of his extortions, but also families of the people he killed) when he got (only) twelve years.

Comment from Ajuoga (Annelies): And the Law will not get evidence that he breaks it. He will not make such a mistake, unless he gets storm in his brain and does the very stupid falling into his own trap. Highly improbable.

Comment from Danced Upon: I wonder how tricky it has been for him to put on the airs of a fully developed man. Do you think he practices looking contemplative and intellectual in front of the mirror as he blow-dries his hair? Maybe he could do commercial work as a caricature of Dorian Gray.

    I had an uncomfortable amount of time on my hands. One morning after putting the pets out in the yard, I got a call from my friend Marcia: "He, him, our GJ, was ranked #2, #3 and #7 on Google this morning when I searched for his name! #7 had two photos of his. All because of our blog!" We were delirious that we had that kind of power. We thought back on all the ways that GJ had duped us and felt justified in gluing him to search engines.

    Surely someone other than us would notice? I realized I had to do more with all the time I had on my hands. I still needed to excavate more of my thoughts and feelings about his lies before I could put it all to rest. There were the glaring untruths that my friends and I scraped off ourselves and threw into what we politely called a pile of refuse. Those were the junk contents of his 'overseas' e-mails, along with the unearthing of years of details told me by the European women.

    Some of the things GJ told me were little white lies meant to make me comfortable. I give him stars for those and I'm grateful that I didn't misread him as a complete rogue. For example, when we were talking about travelling to Greece, he mentioned that all his European women swam and sunbathed topless. I have had a breast reconstruction—which

Walking on Heads

is, by the way, a spectacular specimen—but I have scars and grafted skin and a false nipple. I remember blurting out that I was uncomfortable about flashing my physical cancer story and his gentle response was that two of his exes had inverted nipples and that people didn't pay attention at European beaches like they might in North America. That comment about the beaches was likely true. The one about the twin inversions, though, was likely fictitious, but clearly meant to assure me that I was not an anomaly.

A number of times, GJ talked about a young colleague of his from Rotterdam. He described how Joke—her new name—had once been Joost and had struggled with the sex change, especially the hormonal shifts and the opinions of old friends and some of her family members. He shared this just after Max had invited a friend over to meet us. Grant had been transitioning for a couple of years. GJ also told me several times that Arne and his partner, Alexander, were gay and kept a low profile about it. Also, he mentioned once that his Christian nephew was bisexual, but the rest of the family didn't know about it. These comments could have been true or not, but he was connecting with Max and me by normalizing the fact that my daughter is gay and showing us that it was, for him, not a feature that raised his prejudicial hackles. I thank him for that.

I think that there were also genuine truths. My friends agree that he honestly liked us and appreciated our community of friends, British Columbia and the openness of Canadians. He enjoyed being welcomed and respected by our Vancouver crowd and, while he was here, he portrayed a man filled with tender consideration and appreciation. Perhaps it gave him a sense of the self he yearned for, since one of his needs was to mirror other people, therefore humanizing himself as a moral character. Who knows? We just knew that he wallowed in me, my family, my friends and our community until his lies could no longer be explained.

Nevertheless, there was a profound fog in my head that I needed to clear, because it meant that many of the parts of GJ that I had counted on

GJ is a Trompe l'Oeil

as being true might evaporate and I would have nothing to gasp about anymore. I needed something to attach my indignation to.

Sometimes comments were made, whether true or not, that were just not appropriate and were in hindsight very immature, certainly not the sort of remarks that an educated, mature academic might make. Aside from Caroline (invented so he could participate in my grief) and the fact that he continually misrepresented himself as having assets, there were smaller, yet serrated facts that were also confusing. One day, I returned home to find that one of my spider plants–which had been gloriously healthy when I left—was totally flattened, as if it had fallen on its head. I asked whether he or Dona had knocked it over and he quickly replied, "No!" This was such a childish comeback that I quietly slipped it into my 'Hmmm' file.

There were also sexual comments about the numbers of lovers he had enjoyed as a youth, commentaries about the size of some of his lovers' breasts and muffs . . . including the women I later got to know. He told Jana that Michiel's girlfriend once paraded her half-naked body in front of him trying to give him a lap dance, which Jana and I agreed was likely a sick fantasy of his. These statements would just fly out of left field, and I figure were intended to erode his partner's confidence. The truth could have been that the juvenile quips were more about his wavering, aging libido. Knowing now that he is a broken man, and emotionally close to a boy, explains why he was so immature with many of those careless monologues.

The most tragic lies were those I still do not even know for sure were lies. He said that Arne de Groote was in love with him; that his wife, Anne, was bipolar; that he and his Jewish father had been the best of friends; that he had enjoyed a number of satisfying long-term relationships; and that he had lived in North Africa, Greece, the Antilles, Surinam and Texas. Your guess is as good as mine as to whether any or all of these experiences were true or simply the offshoot of a pathology that demanded he one-up his friends and acquaintances, to appear significantly more sophisticated and evolved than the rest of us.

Walking on Heads

Khalil Gibran wrote, "Beauty is not in the face; beauty is a light in the heart." GJ seemed to struggle with his looks. He disliked that his good looks were falling away, wrestling with the fact that his attractiveness had always been his ticket into a lifestyle he hadn't earned. Some of this may or may not be true. I suspect both. I think that he used—and still uses—his looks, like a hooker child who doesn't quite understand his own abusive performance.

I ramble because so many details are sad, for both his casualties and for GJ as a victim of his biology. I may intellectually understand why he had to lie and be a chameleon, but as I was surfacing from the shock, I didn't want the residues of his survival lies to be like a burr hooking itself into what I had left of my life.

Here's an example of how I realized what I could not have known at the time: I checked his search engine history on my computer occasionally, but he had always cleared it. He did, however, have an impressive list of his own bookmarks that were separate from mine because they were housed in his preferred browser (a different one than I favoured). That, in essence, means that we had separate drawers in the computer for our favourite websites.

It turns out that his research and reading were real, but the poignant part—I am guessing—is that he convinced himself that he was indeed researching for his job and that it was very important work, projecting the belief that he could affect change. It reminded me of the delusions of the man in the book and movie *A Beautiful Mind*.

Not every individual lie or piece of fiction springing from him made for a sociopathic event (though money, travel and fiancée fantasies usually did), but once I started a secondary list, it was blindingly obvious that I should have put an earlier stop to the nonsensical falsehoods that were energetically pushing brokenness on to me. So I wrote a blog entry from the dog's point of view to ease my angst, cloak my judgments and stick my metaphoric finger in his magnificent blue eyes.

GJ is a Trompe l'Oeil

March 28, 2011
Who's at the End of the Leash Now?
(photo of Dona lying by the fireplace)

Posts: 9
Views: 576

As I put my head between my paws, I mull over all the fibs that were thrown like Frisbees at us last fall. When you left, GJ, you dug yourself into a hole deeper than even I could have dug for you. Shall I regurgitate some of the ways you botched it with me?

1. You didn't even say "Goodbye, girl!" or "See you later!" when you fled.
2. How could you make up the white Lipizzan pony, call it the most beautiful animal you had ever seen and post it on your Facebook page? You said I was the beauty!
3. That screwy litany of reasons and explanations as to why you had to go away were like braided cat gut. It took a long time to swallow those strings of fiction and, for those lies, I barf in your general direction.
4. I heard numerous mutterings over that little hand-held computer thing that you were going to Skype with us from Africa. Unless I slept through it, you never called. Dude, that's when I erased you from my friends list.
5. You let people think that you were Anni's guardian angel, but I could see that you had no wings and that there was a little devil in you.
6. My teeth are whiter than yours because I have regular check-ups. And my hair is shinier. I guess that's because you haven't been chased back to your homeland for corrective care.
7. You almost had us, claiming to be an EU observer for the Tanzanian election last fall. I could sense you vibrating at the same frequency as your fiction.

8. We asked about all the wild animals that you said you saw from your Jeep in east Tanzania but we had no reply. That whole scenario smelled queerer than your pungent cologne.
9. Did you ever tell Anni how many long long-distance phone calls you made when she was out? Some were shouted in your funny language ...
10. I have to snoop: how much steak did you eat with the money we lent you, while I only had kibble? The fur will fly if you ever try to come into my yard again.
11. Somali pirates while sailing along the Tanzanian coast, eh? What a Christmas you claimed to have ... except that we all know that what you told us was a load of skunk cabbage.
12. Remember when Anni offered to meet you overseas? Everyone said "No! He won't show up!" and she said, "I know! I'm just playing him ..."
13. We threw out your tennis shoes because, truthfully, even the wintering rat avoided them.
14. You made me sit while you showed me photos of walking trails for us on Saturna Island. The plan smelled fishy, but I sat and faithfully watched anyway.
15. What was that message about returning to continue your research at the University's libraries in Victoria? Even a dog knows that cyberspace is used for searching the literature these days.
16. Did you know that more left-handed people than right-handed ones are sociopaths? I'm ambidextrous and faithful but you are neither.
17. What nerve you have to seriously think that we all believed that you were sent to Mozambique three times—like you're that important?

GJ is a Trompe l'Oeil

18. FYI: Our recycling has reduced considerably. When you were installed here, there were so many empty wine and beer bottles to return. I'm walking with sober people now.
19. What were you thinking? Did you really chew over the idea that you could lose your cellulite and eventually outrun me?
20. Speaking of me again: do you care that I have a new Mister?

Tags: dog smarter than this man
Categories: moral idiot, antisocial personality disorder (ASPD)

Comment from Paralyzed (Marcia): Like all of Danced Upon friends, I had really liked GJ. Now, he reminds me of someone I once thought I knew. He, like GJ, thought he was King Shit but he really was only Fart the messenger boy. Now I know GJ is an ugly Dutch snake ... I wonder when he will be shedding his skin for his next target?

Comment from Danced Upon: What GJ does not 'get' is that WE ARE NOT FOSSILS. We are real sentient beings, on whom he has walked like a public sidewalk. Instead, it is he who is a relic ... a deadbeat ... a spineless object.
Comment from Circe: Wie de bal kaatst, moet hem verwachten. He who bounces the ball, must expect it back.

19

Tennis, Anyone?

Wise men talk because they have something to say; fools because they have to say something.
— Plato —

Looking back, there were even more details that made no sense. A few tidbits didn't come to my memory centre until much later—at least, not until I started talking about them. I dredged up bits and pieces one at a time like an archaeologist, yet thankfully, I didn't lose any sleep. I think that memory can be protective, only letting elements slip at a pace we can handle and process them.

One flashback that popped up, like one of my student's hands in class, came as I was driving by a local tennis club in the posh Point Grey area of Vancouver. I saw a couple of ladies carrying their gear and wearing their tennis whites.

I remembered that GJ had played—not at that exclusive club, but with a few guys out at the university courts. He had told me that court time was free to staff and that he was playing with a couple of faculty members he had met through Marie.

One man had, in fact, picked him up at the house a couple of times, and I heard that they were very good at doubles. I had only spoken briefly to faculty Sam because of my emotional fragility at the time, but I knew

Walking on Heads

his full name and I had noticed that he was a friend of GJ's on Facebook. Those two tennis warriors were so good that Sam had enrolled the duo in a doubles tournament in Richmond and they had practiced often, spiritedly determined to place well.

Two uncanny things clinked into place when I recollected one of the stories I had been spoon-fed by my professional liar. One was that Sam was no longer on GJ's Facebook friends list. And the second (aha!) was that GJ had claimed that he had re-damaged a running injury by slipping on a rock at the beach just before the tournament and never did get to participate in the competition. Looking back, his moans about his leg had been louder than Nat's had been when she was in great pain . . . and I had to question if there had ever been a wound, a stint in a cross-country race or anything more physical in his life than his recreational sports and his pursuit of women.

So, gutsy as I'd become, I messaged Sam, noting that he and GJ had severed their friendship and wondering (gulp) if it had anything to do with money.

By the next day I had the answer I expected. It had everything to do with money! GJ owed Sam personally for paying their doubles tournament fees, as well as their contribution for many weeks' worth of court rentals. Indeed, GJ's words to Sam time after time had been "I'll take care of it!" The man had walked on yet another person!

I wrote the next blog partly to get under Mr. Jank's skin, should he ever catch on to us. Barbra said that she had a photo of him naked on a tennis court, doing his famous left-handed serve, but we didn't want to risk offending readers. However, I knew that any reference to his looks would drive him crazy. It was true, he was losing his movie star exterior, and I didn't mind saying so for all of us. After all, he had played tennis with our hearts and our bank accounts.

Tennis, Anyone?

March 28, 2011   Posts: 10
Tennis, Anyone?   Views: 653

In the game of life, do we win some and lose some? Do drop shots or foot faults effect the outcome of our daily 'games'?

Silly questions! Odd, but also compulsory for us, because there are cheaters in life who see their advances and style as part of their personal sport. They manipulate and position their games according to their own rules. They—or in this case, Goos Jank—put spins on stories that in the long run have us, the targets, sweating and winded inside, unaware that a game is being played out.

Backhanded comments and lobs to cause us to lose inner balance and belief in ourselves are all part of the strategy to win the game against the innocent player. But our guy doesn't have big enough balls. Nor does he have a decent drop shot anymore, because he's losing his conditioning, his toned body and his fine legs. And he's not so easy to watch in the game because of sun damage and bad feet. Finding innocent players may be getting harder for him. Others need to know that he is incapable of getting to set point, never mind 'love'.

Can we allow deception as well as immorality and uncertainty to be volleyed in our lives anymore? As we speak up against what cruelly dishonourable plays have been made on the court of life, we become the challengers and we have the advantage of being able to hit a flatliner ball at him with serious speed. Together, we can end his game and its unsportsmanlike moves and surprise him with our own double and triple hits.

He's sick, and he's going out of this game, because we are practicing our own sport and we have the aces we need.

Walking on Heads

Tags: cheater, player
Categories: sociopath, immorality, pathological lying

Comment from Linsey: I thought "Tennis Anyone?" was a brilliant piece ... the problem with 'like' is that you have to sign up for your own blog ... it is an uphill climb for this not computer-savvy friend. Anyway, I LIKED IT!

Love, L

Comment from Mark Jones: Googled Mr. Jank. Found this site. I have not been able to contact him yet but I have some questions. I worked with Jank in the Balkans in the early 2000s. We were both there in an official capacity. Met him at monthly SID meetings and rest assured: you only get in there having a very official accreditation. That does not tally with your story at all. And I met up with him last year in Zanzibar at a conference where on invitation, he gave a quite impressive presentation. Dear sir/lady, parts of your story are, apart from very contradictory, simply not true. Sounds to me you are a rejected lover, and I know how bad and messy that can feel.

Nevertheless, as a former blogger, I realise you blatantly violate the code of conduct which prohibits personal attacks on a private person (whether there is truth in it or not). I will certainly report this on the complaints site.

Regards, Mark

Comment from Danced Upon: Thank you, Mr. Jones. We know how difficult it can be to try to Google Goos, as he has no work history in cyberspace nor a stable land address. You can, however, find him on Facebook, along with a current e-mail address. It's a pity you didn't pick up his business card when you shared space at his presentation in Stone Town—last year, was it? Your name sounds Welsh but your syntax is interesting. Are you perhaps European?

Regards, P

Comment from Big Fish: Danced Upon, light me up a bit . . . Welsh name but not the Welsh syntax. Do you refer to Mr. Jones' stating: "I have not been able to contact GJ yet but I have some questions" . . . after which he didn't raise any question nor formed any phrase ending with a question mark? I don't know for Welsh, but all Europeans regularly use a question mark.

Comment from Big Fish: For a moment I felt to 'represent' Europeans and their writing grammar in an essay, "European Question Marks Worldwide!" Although I have not been QUITE ACCREDITED by the Association for the Correct Application of EU Grammatics, every European knows how to be clear on the subject of the what is the question and to end the inquiry with a question mark.

Now, seriously . . . I really didn't understand what this Mister Jones wrote about and what he is complaining about. It seems to me, but I may be in error, he states he personally met a GJ officially accredited by the SID! I spent time with GJ in the Balkans and I do not remember his accreditation with any group, except the tennis club.

If Mister Jones is not a spammer or troll himself, he threatens to signal an 'abuse" asking for a suspension of a personal attack blog. Obviously, he is free to submit the form, but this blog DOESN'T threat any real, honest legitimate person, doesn't call to violence and ...ABOVE ALL ... not one of us impersonates another private person!

The use of nicknames is not explicitly prohibited by the blog. The bloggers are using them for their own protection. Behind our nicknames are real persons who don't impersonate anybody else but themselves, under the nickname. All our comments are clearly against violence and in favour of victims of frauds and abuses. It seems to me Mister Jones misunderstood not only the purpose but also the word 'abuse'. Besides, I simply don't understand WHAT EXACTLY 'TOUCHED' HIM SO MUCH? Did somebody catch his point and will you explain it to me?

20

Once a Cheater, Always a Cheater

A man wrapped up in himself makes a very small bundle.

— John Ruskin —

We outed GJ—less than a month into our blogging, we'd had our first unknown person remark. We were imbibing cocktails with shots of bewilderment, elation, anger and fear. As the administrator, I had the option of accepting or moderating the 'Mark Jones' comment, so I copied and e-mailed it to the sisterhood and waited for their directions before either Jana or I commented back. Jana suggested that we play nice and try to draw him out. I had to phone Bryn and Ev, who were patently upset by his attempt at presenting himself as a good man concerned about another good man. I was stunned by the man's use of the word *rejected*.

The girls calmed me down, saying that 'rejected' was part of his story, not the real story. 'Mark Jones' was a man-boy needing to lash out at being found out. I felt like a little girl until Team Anni reminded me that his words were purposefully poisonous.

So, sticks and stones may break our bones, but words were not going to hurt us. Two pages of e-mails later, we had gigantic—albeit uncomfortable—amusement at knowing that it was him! First, the Mark fellow said that he'd Googled GJ, but in my admin stats on the blog site there were

Walking on Heads

no search engine pingbacks on that day using GJ's name. However, there had been a search done using the words 'left-handed' and 'sociopath'. Second, the critic Mark exploited GJ's own favoured term, 'messy'. Third, he'd designed a similar e-mail address to GJ's. 'GoosJ1955@thefree-mail.com' sure looks like 'markjones1966@thefree-mail.com'. GJ certainly may have been shrewd, but the jerk lacked imagination.

There's a fourth, a fifth and a sixth detail. GJ had never been out of Canada to speak in Tanzania last year, because I knew he was in overstay of his visitor's visa (never mind the fact that he was with me, because he moved in with me just after Nathalie's death)! And Barbra sent a startled and angry e-mail message: "In 2000, Goosjerk was living with me in Zeist, Netherlands!" And finally, what an ego to strut: the man had supposedly delivered "a quite impressive speech," which sounded very parallel to GJ's own description of his imaginary presentation in the Hague in the fall when he claimed to have "delivered an inspired, maybe provocative speech". That resemblance was glaring and hilarious.

Understandably, I had two new blog posts ready within a few days to nurse that ranting comment.

March 30, 2011   Posts: 11
Dear Mr. Jank   Views: 754

Dear Mr. Goos Dickensheets Jank,

It is with modest regret that we send this letter to inform you that you are no longer a person of interest. We understand that you had requested to work in our organization. Although your personal contact made an appealing first impression, we are looking for someone not only more qualified, but also with a spotless history.

Your CV as a Ph.D, a man of character and a man with integrity has been rejected. Your academic references were

Once a Cheater, Always a Cheater

not available. Your personal references did not offer glowing accounts of particular behaviours. Sharing how your sons watched you have a vasectomy is not acceptable during an employment interview.

We need a team player, a person who can do what he says he will when he says it will be dealt with. We are looking for someone with a history of genuine dialoguing and sound skills with money.

There is sparse evidence that you can go the distance. You have not had stable addresses, any work history, a relationship with a bank or any credit history to assure us that you are who you say you are. The only evidence we could find about your community-based 'work' came from an anti-fraud romance scammer website.

Your file, Mr. Jank, will receive a 'BROKEN' report, because there have been people in your life who have loved you and who have welcomed you into their lives. We feel that you have some innate qualities that are worthy of your submission being forwarded to a healing institution... outside of Canada.

Reference #1955, March 2011

Tags: lying about credentials
Categories: cheater, pathological liar, sociopath

Comment from Linsey: The humour is helpful to clarify how many ways GJ has lied and used people to his own ends... it really is pathological... our natures as healthy human beings are geared towards finding ways to understand others... usually this leads to affinity and compassion... unfortunately, betrayed natures have a hard time working through the betrayal and coming to terms with it at some level so we can live our lives without malice and distrust... good work, Danced Upon, for keeping your head up... our sisterhood is not isolated... we are strong and united in finding ways to inform and hopefully protect others from Mr. Jank and others like him.

* * *

March 31, 2011   Posts: 12
Jilted?   Views: 852

Anyone who has followed the *Cruel Bastaard* blog and comments can clearly see that this site is about double-crossing and the swindling of trust.

The truth is that the loss of GJ from each of the bloggers' lives was about him passing his point of no return with us. We have compared notes, and each of us could not wait to see the back of him as he packed up and slid out the metaphorical door from our lives.

What did we lose? Aside from the money that he had assured us he would recompense and the headaches we had from the twists in his stories and his plans, trust became the greatest write-off, because we learned the hard way that some people are not honourable with their emotions, words, assurances and their stories.

I played GJ's game for a while last year when he claimed he was in Zanzibar working for the Dutch government (but was instead in Toronto, working on his next make-believe project). I played along, waiting for his concocted replies. The only part of the game that he controlled was when and if he would return. A part of me wanted him to come back, if only because I wanted my money back, and then I wanted to kick his flat ass while sending him on his way out my back gate.

Once a Cheater, Always a Cheater

Perhaps, if anyone has ever felt jilted in their relationships, it is Goos Jank himself who has suffered cold rejection from a variety of beautiful, successful women who have said "Enough!"

Tags: double-crosser, swindler
Categories: pathological lying, sociopath

Comment from Circe: Bravo. Glad to wash my hands from him.

21
Abcdefg

Looks fade, but dumb is forever.
— Judge Judy Sheindlin —

I thought that I was running out of indignation, until the Mark Jones comment. GJ was either stepping on the nasty pedal or reverting to a childish pattern of throwing the kitchen sink at anyone daring to critique him. He was living out the profile of an antisocial personality. I likely fit the profile of a self-indulgent woman, but I carried on with our creative righteous anger, knowing that it would pull at his short hairs.

By coincidence, I was checking my social networks, ploughing through old messages and deleting some, especially the old planning messages that had been sent for Nathalie's Celebration of Life. That's when I remembered that there was a new name for a friend in my message box, next to all the old messages sent from GJ. The barmy man had changed his name. I say 'barmy' because the social network in question allows for only one name change. Instead of just making up a new account with a new name, he kept his old profile, doubtless for his extensive friends list—which meant he would need to explain to everyone why he had altered both his first name and his surname to become Gerlach Jaeger.

Walking on Heads

Because 'Anni Mills' was blocked from seeing his profile information, I opened a new account under my maiden name and given first name. This was my way to at least see what GJ was allowing people to see. The only things visible to non-friends were photos, but yes, there were six pictures of our man! His wall and info were blocked, but the photo taken by Jana in Italy and several taken by Marie were assembled. Also, when I checked a few of his old friends through my maiden name, I noticed that they had a new/old friend named Gerlach.

I have tripped over myself about this and you might have to grasp social networking to appreciate my conundrum. Two separate and carefully selected options murmured at me as to how he would explain away his name change to all of his friends. The simplest reason he could share with his flock of followers, as far as I could figure, was his choice to become a German citizen because of his German bloodlines—which supersede residency and birthplace in terms of applying for citizenship—and that he had adopted his father's German name. He is such a talented storyteller that he could have made that decision make sense to his allies.

What felt like a snakebite for me, however, was the fact that Goos or Gerlach, or whatever his alter-ego was that day, had also possibly divulged, at least to his closest friends, that he was being pursued by an unhinged and sick woman, or even a group of ridiculous ex-lovers (although a whole posse of crazy women might have been hard for even his closest long-term friends to swallow).

Somehow, however, Marie did not show up on any of the friends lists of Gerlach Jaeger, or in the pictures of our Goos. This made me wonder if he was possibly claiming to be harangued by a woman, but that person was not me or one of us, but Marie! He had dissected parts of her professional backbone and pasted them to his own profile. I just had to visit the possibility that someone else, if not Marie, was also on to Goos. There was also the chance that she was defending his name change and his reasons for it, although that felt like my imagination had

Abcdefg

become hysterically over-productive. This was all an intricate jumble in my mind because a number of her friends used to be his friends and I wondered how he could explain the name change to their mutual friends and if, as he persisted in living off her, her friends and her children might have possibly picked up a strange scent. Several of Marie's companions would have been academics. Wouldn't someone have figured out that GJ's theoretical and scholarly posturing might be punky?

April 1, 2011   Posts: 13
Ice People   Views: 1000
(GJ squinting in the sun with Dona)

Here is Goos, sitting innocently in our garden last summer in British Columbia. Like a boy, he is wearing his favourite and most worn T-shirt from the University of Toronto. He claimed that this shirt came from attending a Ph.D conference on leadership. But he is an April Fool. He does not have leadership credentials or a leadership work history. In fact, he 'borrowed' the shirt from his roommate and kept it for the six months he sponged off of me.

Posting this blog is helping us four women recover from being his prey, as the objects of his charismatic appetite. GJ professes to be educated, solvent, honourable and faithful. His disguise is laced with charm and the adopted experiences which set him up to receive money, lodging, gifts and kindness from vulnerable women in a very calculated way.

Unfortunately, he is dead man in his heart. Anyone who does not own a conscience or true feelings is emotionally dead. GJ may look, act, dress and emote as if he is principled, but he is without the capacity to be fully alive without borrowing or seizing others' lives and opinions and memories.

He is like a wolf in sheep's clothing, wanting desperately to be soft and fuzzy.

Walking on Heads

Say it isn't so! He seemed like a genuinely nice man. He exuded warmth and intelligence, assuring our families and our friends that we were in good company. But his blood must be sludgy like melting frost. Otherwise, how could he continually choose to chase down intelligent, trusting women and then dash away when his appetite has been sated?

Instead, GJ is an ice person and an emotional idiot.
Great legs? Check.
Beautiful eyes? Check!
Cold heart? Check.

Tags: wolf in sheep's clothing
Categories: pathological lying, sociopath

Comment from Circe: And the T-shirt . . . as if exchanging personalities . . . it proves his powerful influence and manipulations in love fraud. I sent WhatsHERname a warning, doing good for another human being in danger. She did not want to be bothered! She blocked me on Facebook. I hope GJ will marry her and we all will be safe from the madman. But he will ruin her and drain her, that vampire man.

Comment from Linsey: I think the details from the blog are helpful to clarify how many ways GJ has lied and used people to his own ends . . . he really is a moral idiot . . . but . . . we are not isolated . . . we are strong and united.

Comment from Danced Upon: Is cheating not the same as embezzling? I'm pretty sure that GJ hadn't dealt drugs or taken an old lady's life savings (although it is possible). He did not rob stockholders of millions and he didn't operate like a Nigerian romance scammer . . . at least with us. BUT, cheating on your

Abcdefg

lover is cheating whether it's taking money, trust or good will. In all cases, the unsuspecting are not conscious of the icy, premeditated sting.

Comment from Margot Ritter: What a funny blog you have, Danced Upon! First I thought it was all about this GJ, but now I realize it is all about you! It is all about your compulsive obsession with this undoubtedly fascinating (good or bad) man! Get real: he left you for someone else. Always messy, hardly ever ethical. Love is cruel. But no, you want revenge: the wrath and anger of an abandoned lover. You say you want to save the world from this devil and warn innocent women! Haha! And then as the ultimate argument you use the death of your daughter and your own cancer to make us feel sorry for you. You should be ashamed of yourself. From every line you write there oozes sheer negativity and diabolical anger! If that is the mission of your life, I pity you. But I doubt you even have lost a child or have cancer! And then there is this Big Fish person. Real or not, she, just like you, incoherently rants and raves as if she is the personification of the devil as depicted in "RoseMarie's Baby."

Best, Margot Ritter.

    The second comment made from a stranger to our blog (supposedly from a woman) had a familiar writing style and could only have been written by GJ (who misspelled Rosemary, ironically with 'Marie' in it). His fury was partly in response to a piece that I had posted called "The C Word."
    In that very personal blog, which I cannot share, I mused over how GJ reminded me of my cancer. I was clear in the piece that the great tragedy of my life was the loss of my daughter, whereas the morality of GJ was just plain wrong and twisted. Surprisingly, it was not that I thought he

made my cancer exponentially worse. In fact, what the experience with him had done was bring the term 'fight' into the forefront of my mind. I recognized that his sickness needed to be stopped and fought.

I wrote that I do not hate the man, just as I do not hate my cancer. However, I made the point that I was uneasy and exasperated by what he had done and by how his offenses had multiplied. While I still had breath, I stated that even if it put my life in danger through the threat of retribution, I would continue to write about what Goos Jank had done to innocent people, including his own children.

First of all, if a real woman had happened upon and read even a couple of our blog entries and comments about the abuse that we tolerated—most particularly if she had read "The C Word"—there was no way that she would berate another woman so callously in her comments. Why would she even do that if she didn't know any of us?

Even if the critical 'Margot' was not a mother, unless she herself suffered from ASPD, she would never enter the territory of the loss of a child. And furthermore, who signs cruel and nasty comments with 'best'? Instead, it was him escalating and getting very angry that we were calling the shots.

I was about to comment back that Johnny couldn't read and neither could Margot, when the blog was suspended. I was pissed off that he was so foul, knowing how deeply his statements would hurt me. I wanted to have the last hurrah! I don't know what else I wanted, but it felt incomplete.

Barbra did have words for us, however. She e-mailed us:

> You know his thinking. You have sharp strategy minds. He indeed wanted to shoot. He shot out Danced Upon is fake, no cancer, no passed away daughter and that Big Fish is fake. But he could not try with me that I am 'fake'. We all have the right to express our positive and negative feelings and that is the purpose of this blog to have such an exchange of thoughts. But, I am a bit more quiet now knowing he will attack . . . he will not give up.

Abcdefg

> This is what worries me. Marie will give him money and he will look to get us with more than calling names.

Subsequently, the responses from GJ had the effect he wanted. We had been silenced and immobilized. Jana was fit to be tied, raving mad but still on edge because, although he had compared her to the demon in *Rosemary's Baby*, he was still pursuing her with e-mails. Barbra had been anxious and wanting us to shut the blog down since the 'Mark Jones' comment and was wringing her hands, practically looking over her shoulders. Annelies was troubled about his pathology and concerned about how this blogging was affecting my health. For my part, I was starting to see spooks behind my shrubs, which could be blamed on the sudden number of spam e-mails I was receiving on the topics of finding soul mates, heart-matches, sex clubs and new lovers, thinking that he might be insulting and goading me.

As a matter of fact, one evening I heard my smartphone ring and I ran and grabbed it without looking at the caller. A man's voice asked, "Anneee? This is Darren [MacSomething]. Would Gerry be there?" I said, "Pardon me?" and the voice repeated his request, although the second time it sounded more like he was looking for a ghost. I stuttered that he must have had the wrong number as I quickly hit 'END'.

Maxine was playing with the cat in the living room and, when I told her about the weird call she suggested I trace it, but it was from an unknown number and I didn't have the nerve to call it back. I had to wonder if it might be a friend of Marie's in the hunt for GJ, now known as Gerlach Jaeger.

As far as I knew, GJ was still in Canada and maybe heading back to British Columbia with Marie, who may have been returning to her work with Langara College. I had been afraid that GJ might show up at the house and for a while I carried my cordless house phone with the 9-1-1 emergency number on speed dial whenever someone rang the doorbell.

Then, I sweated about the safety of my daughter. Along with that angst, I wondered if GJ might just burn my house down, knowing how

Walking on Heads

terrified I am of fire. The last neurotic thought I had, just as the blog was suspended, was that he would come to the park where Dona and I regularly walked and strangle me or her behind a tree.

To regain my balance, I generated and played with a number of far-fetched fantasies. In fact, my friends and I bounced a few around. I imagined that as GJ was driving back to BC to get me, en route he would trip into a mire of broom bushes and sneeze himself into a coma, or thought that while peeing by the side of the road in the Rocky Mountains, a mudslide might carry him away. I visualized him soon losing all his hair, having developed alopecia from worry about being Googled. I pictured GJ being lynched by the brothers, partners and male friends of the women hurt by him. I anticipated that the bags under his eyes would become so atrocious that no woman would ever want him again. I had fun pretending that Lorena Bobbitt would stalk him, or that he would at least become impotent, that his teeth would fall out and his nose hairs become chronically infected. Lastly, I hoped that someone might recognize him or at least his type from the *Cruel Bastaard* blog parts that were still accessible and floating around indefinitely in cyberspace.

My support team didn't collapse with the crash of the blog, though. Jana and my friend Linsey both wrote to the blog administrator requesting a reassessment of his or her decision. Linsey shared hers with the sisters, and we gave our brave women high-fives for being so proactive as we celebrated having invited over two thousand views in the month that we had been dynamically blogging.

> This e-mail is an appeal of your decision to suspend the *Cruel Bastaard* blog, and I request that it go to a manager for consideration. Speaking as a commenter on the blog I would ask you to consider the implications of your 'personal attack' rule on victims of sociopaths or psychopaths . . . I accept that this is a delicate issue and that you have to protect your reputation and integrity . . . however in this

Abcdefg

particular instance, the actual 'attacker' is the subject of the blog, and the person who was violated through lies, manipulation, fraud (both personal and financial) is acting not to attack but to stand up for herself and to warn other potential prey as best she can ... The problem for women who have been victimized is the very real danger of being identified and then victimized again .... so your rule about anonymity, while completely valid and laudable for the vast majority, will actually enable the victimizer to silence their victim. Society and the legal system do not and cannot protect those wounded by sociopaths unless there has been some overt and provable violence ... the friends of Danced Upon were optimistic that her ability to voice and expose her exploitation would help her heal and also help protect other women ... the blog was the medium of choice.

Is there some way that I could stand by the words on the blog with my real name such that the victim can maintain her blog's intention of warning and supporting other women in danger and still protect your website's integrity? I am seriously concerned that the silencing of victims' voices by a blog site sets a dangerous precedent and requires some serious understanding of the issues and full consideration of the consequences of your decision for victims. I would appreciate hearing your thoughts regarding my appeal.

Yours respectfully,
Linsey D.

Oddly, however, once the blog was terminated because of Mark's appeal to the blog host and the dust had settled, I felt calm and collected. Neither Linsey nor Jana ever received replies to their petitions. But I

Walking on Heads

did! The blog administration's standard e-mail response to me explained simply that I would have to choose another venue for my fight because personal critiques, brought to their attention, were not allowed.

Fair enough.

We had done what we wanted to do—there was nothing left to blog about. We could let GJ think that he had won. We didn't care because we had gotten to him! I had managed to have him investigated for overstay of his visitor's visa and for possibly hacking into the blog site's servers. He had been forced to change his name because Goos had been exposed as a walking trespasser. His picture and name were submitted to a romance scammers website. Marie may have followed him or vouched for him, but we didn't care how much he walked all over her. However, she is welcome to join our sisterhood should she need our support and understanding.

22
The Fine Print

There's a sucker born every minute.
—P.T. Barnum—

I had one more post left up my sleeve before we were suspended. Unlike that fake comment from the woman Margot, those of us in the sisterhood with real estrogen were howling with laughter at GJ's attempt to cross-dress his persona. This last post, based on an unmoderated or unapproved comment from a woman called Anne Beren, was drafted but never had a chance for authorization or posting by me as the administrator because of the swift suspension of the *Cruel Bastaard* blog.

> Unposted Views: 0
> *The Fine Print.* This note was sent by a woman who has been nicknamed 'Runaway Rose' for her protection.

It is risky what you are doing, but very brave to strike a blow for women everywhere. Be careful, this man will still try to take from you. He will try to convince others that you were the witches and that he was done wrong. He thinks that the sun rises for free.

And he will only admit defeat when cats lay goose eggs. My advice is let it go.

It is, however, a pity that men do not come with fine print, like a bank contract. That way, women would know what the risks would be. I send warm compliments and warnings as I share with you a checklist from an article which was a help to me.

There's Fungus Amongus:
1. Do you ever feel used, emotionally, financially or physically?
2. Have you frequently felt that the person doesn't really, actually care about you?
3. Has he/she ever misled or misinformed you?
4. Has the individual made contradictory statements that confuse you?
5. Do you sometimes feel he/she has taken advantage of your generous nature?
6. Does he/she often use flattery or smooth talk even if he/she says nothing blatantly or genuinely complimentary?
7. Have his/her actions or lack of reactions made you feel worried?
8. Does the person chronically fail to take responsibility, instead pointing his finger at everyone and everything but himself?

I suppose that one victory is that this piece was sent by a real person who supported and cared about us. We think that it might have even been GJ's ex-wife.

Even though the points she left us with did not get broadcasted, the statements made us think about the other sociopaths we may have rubbed shoulders with in our lives. Dr. Hare from the University of British

The Fine Print

Columbia claims that each of us, every day, may brush by someone with pathological inclinations.

Our obligation is to trust our intuition. Illusions can come in all kinds of forms, some crafted as art and some in the form of skewed, crafty people.

I think I had a boss once who fit the profile sent by Anne Beren.

23

Exit Stage Left

Life is like music; it must be composed by ear, feeling and instinct, not rules.

— Samuel Butler —

Our blog was shut down for violating one of the blog site's terms of service. We were told that we had made the blog a personal attack.

My mantra throughout this recovery from being heartlessly violated was buried deep within my psyche. Even I didn't know that I was driven by the saying 'No rest for the wicked'. I truly believed that the path away from my shock and dismay was to heal collectively with GJ's other casualties.

If I hadn't found my international sisters, I know in my heart that I would have chalked up the thefts to experience and that I would have moved on, I would never have realized that GJ was a sociopath, or even known what that was! When I came up against the clearly dreadful things that he had done to each one of us, I knew that I could no longer stay quiet.

The reality is that GJ's wrongdoings to us were very personal. His lies involved our families, our time, our trust, our money and to varying degrees, our reputations. Still, the glaring fact that has distressed me the most, amongst a cluster of traits shared by sociopaths, is the characteristic embezzling of wholesome emotions and the transferring of them to themselves, without an emotional scaffold to sustain such sentiments for long.

Furthermore, it was unbelievably cruel that GJ used the death of my daughter to create a parallel story so that I would feel sorrow and guilt for him and his made-up loss. That was inexcusable! And for that alone I stand behind my decision to make it personal. Indeed, it was personal from the beginning. It just took me time to figure out how very, very personal it was.

As far as forgiveness goes, I accept that GJ's disease has left him short on the morals and the qualities that we expect from others. I do think that he tried to act like a good partner while he was living with me, but his lies about his past made it crucial for him to lie even more, which unquestionably caused inner vertigo for me and my circle of family and friends. Even his use of my daughter's illness and then death was not something he rubbed his hands together over and thought, *Here's a ripe one!* I believe that his warped mind attempted the appearance of caring and, if creating a parallel story generated that sensation of compassion, I guess it's what his juvenile self with its arrested development had to do.

If I go back to the cruel comments by Mark and Margot, I see how the dangerous GJ sounded off like air-raid horns because his brokenness could not handle the truth, finally mislaying his choirboy charm. I can't speak for how nasty he had been with his sons, his family, the women I chanced upon or the swath of victims left in his slipstream.

I feel very, very sorry for him and his particular type of scammer, who are merely purposeless knick-knacks, and my own form of forgiveness is personal. Still, I would do it all again and 'Droste' him back, returning the mind-twisting, recursive tactic to its owner for walking all over my motherhood.

I realize that there could be some fallout from this story. Sociopaths do not like to be exposed and there will possibly be allegations that I have made this all up and that I have been irrationally vindictive as a discarded lover. My losses, as one can imagine, are monumental. As a mother, I had

Exit Stage Left

to watch my eldest daughter die, and I know that my youngest daughter is watching me fade. When one knows one is dying, there is no comfort in retribution or proving one's brilliance. At least for me, my only comfort is love. I have written this story in the most loving way I could, but as in playing a serious game of cards, I have played my hand well.

GJ's pretended devotion to me is not a significant loss, but his actions were absurdly feculent and sour. If he had not actually grifted from me, I would never have wasted my remaining precious time making up such an ugly story to validate my life. Sociopaths are expert in convincing others that their accusers are daft, but although I am failing, my mind is so far still sound.

The second piece of fallout from my storytelling may be some ducking and diving from those who have been complicit in the covering up of GJ's indiscretions. There may be some guilt and denial on their part, but that is their own business.

Was it wrong to go public and expose GJ? Sometimes I have thought that it was a wicked thing to do, but I know that it was not nearly as fiendish as what he has done to others. I have unveiled my story to hold up the heart placard for those abandoned either by death or by deceit. Sharing my rebelliousness as my counterpoint to fraud is what I wanted to do for the Nathalies and Maxines of the world, as a demonstrative template for why indecent behaviours thrust at us are calls for proactivity.

I do not regret giving myself to GJ, but in the long run it was I who decided how much he could take from me. So you see, dear reader: all choices can have a beginning, a middle and an end.

Acknowledgments

Where to start? How about with my Grandmother Brown and my Aunty Poppy who instilled in me a love of reading. And to my parents who encouraged me from childhood to write, whether letters to Walt Disney or thank-you letters to my family in response to gifts. It was all good training. Then, I'll throw in the Sister lecturer from Brescia College who roused my concentration so that I aced my reading and writing assignments in English literature.

And scooping my mind from my past, my lovers were always pretty proud of all the newspaper columns I pounded out for no pay. And, of course, my heart is forever grateful for Geneviève and Lara, who proved that the experience of motherhood was the best breeding ground for growing up and being truly accountable.

As far as my experiences and the aftermath of the *anni horribili* (horrible years) that I went through regarding illness, death and treachery, I have the following dear people to thank, in alphabetical order so not to offend anyone. Love and kisses to Alaya, Alexandra, Anne, Arielle, Bronia, Claude, Derek, Don, Ellen, Jeff, Jeanette, Gosia, Linda,

Lynn, Nadina, Noelle, Nelly, Patrice, Philip, Sandy, Sara, Sophie, Shona, Triona, Vicki and Zeta. Thanks also to the compassionate staff at the B.C. Cancer Agency and the commandingly kind teams from the Vancouver Coastal Home Care Nursing units and St. Mary's Hospital.

Pretending that I'm having an Academy Award moment, I'd like to also thank all the friends and family of the above-mentioned people as well as the staff I had the honour to work along with for years as part of the Vancouver Coastal Health public health team. These incredible people know who they are.

Muffin Soup: the Discovered Words of Art of Geneviève Gaulin

www.muffinsoup.com

words

Words on a page
fractured thoughts
sometimes they grow like
plants, like they're alive
I can watch them

※

Muffin Soup

Maybe you should try it, the innocent life.
You may find yourself returning to childhood forever.

After Geneviève's passing, boxes of journals, scribbles, poetry, art and words of wisdom were found. Several of these pieces have been collected for a website created in her honour.

Echo

Music and lyrics by Lara Matiation, in memory of her sister, Geneviève, who passed away March 22, 2010.

I am so weak since you've been gone. I have been beat but carry on.
It's hard to find the strength myself, to not depend on someone else.
Your words echo through me.

Chorus:
Don't worry and waste your time, just hurting every day and night,
still searching for another life, while the one you're in passes you by.
You were the one who showed me, life is what you make it out to be.
You can always wear a smile, put it on and you're in style.
Your words echo through me.

Goodbye! While I know that it isn't right when someone leaves too soon.
You don't have to see it, to believe it.
Faith is up to you.
Even though I'm on my own, I know that I'm not alone.
Your words echo through me.

© 2010 Lara Matiation

www.facebook.com/matiationmusic
www.twitter.com/matiationmusic

Topics for Discussion

1. Consider some of the book's themes. For example, how important are the topics of:

    - Art
    - Denial
    - Family
    - Forgiveness
    - Friendships
    - Innocence
    - Irony
    - Isolation
    - Loss
    - Love
    - Lies
    - Masks
    - Motherhood
    - Power
    - Sexual Orientation
    - Social Networking

2. If one (or more) of the characters made a choice that had moral implications, would you have made the same decision? Why? Why not?

3. What types of images does the author create with the names she has chosen for some of her characters?

4. Why do you think that the author had chosen to write the story as a novel?

5. Have you ever met or dealt with a person like GJ?

6. How did Anni and some of the other characters change or evolve over the course of the narrative? What events triggered such changes?

7. Which of GJ's actions were the results of freedom of choice or of nature vs nurture?

8. How are the narrator's emotions symbolically significant?

9. Did the book end the way you expected?

10. Would you recommend this book to other readers? Would you pass it on to your best friend?

Dania Matiation was born in Toronto, Ontario in a year with two nines in it. She studied at the University of Western Ontario and the University of Guelph before moving to Edmonton to intern in dietetics. She later settled on the west coast of British Columbia.

Dania worked for many years as a nutritionist for Vancouver Coastal Health, also speaking extensively on critical issues in her field and writing articles on food, nutrition and family dynamics.

She authored *Food Swings*, about the personal relationship each of us has with food, and *Motherwords*, which imparted words of wisdom to her children. *Walking on Heads* is based on her own experience with a pathological liar and some of the others he deceived.

Dania did indeed lose her daughter exactly as the story tells. She, too, was challenged to live with the same incurable diagnosis and passed away in early December, 2011. Despite her cancer, she persevered, and with her wit, tenacity and good humour was able to complete this book.